STRATEGIC THINKING FOR ADVERTISING CREATIVES

STRATEGIC THINKING FOR ADVERTISING CREATIVES

ALICE KAVOUNAS TAYLOR

LAURENCE KING PUBLISHING

This book is dedicated to my wonderful students who rightly accused me of repeating myself about the importance of strategy, then learned it so well that they've become creatives all over the world.

LAURENCE KING

Published in 2013 by Laurence King Publishing Ltd
361-373 City Road
London EC1V 1LR
United Kingdom

Tel: +44 20 7841 6900
Fax: +44 20 7841 6910

email: enquiries@laurenceking.com
www.laurenceking.com

Published in 2013 by
Laurence King Publishing Ltd

A catalogue record for this book is available from the British Library.

ISBN: 978-1-78067-273-1

Design: TwoSheds Design
Senior editor: Peter Jones
Jacket illustration: Billie Jean

Printed in China

CONTENTS

'STRATEGY IS 70% OF CREATIVITY.'

Dan Watts, Fallon

INTRODUCTION

The quote opposite by Dan Watts, a leading creative at Fallon, might surprise you. Isn't strategy someone else's job? After all, you're creative. The aim of this book is to give you a springboard for your creativity: an understanding of strategic thinking. Because, as Dan's quote indicates, the ability to think strategically lies at the heart of true creativity.

This book is written and designed for you, the creative person heading for an advertising agency. Perhaps you're already there, eager to tackle every brief that comes your way. Whichever type of agency it is, integrated, digital, traditional, small or large, local or global, you, the creative person, are central to its survival. Your creativity is the spark that ignites the pitch meeting. Your creativity translates into the agency's overall ability to win and keep accounts. Of course every department is important, but without a creative department, you're not really talking about an ad agency. The brilliance, as well as the consistency, of your creative work, will determine your career path and your success. And strategy is, as Dan says, 70 per cent of that creativity.

WHAT IS STRATEGY?

You hear the word 'strategy' used all the time. You probably know that it originated as a military term. The *Collins Millennium Edition Dictionary* defines strategy as 'the art or science of the planning and conduct of a war'. The second definition gets closer to what we need to work with: 'a particular long-term plan for success, esp. in business or politics'. And finally, the third definition of strategy is simply: 'a plan'.

So in broad terms a 'strategy' is a plan. But not just any old plan. It's a tactical plan, carefully thought through to enable you to achieve your objective. Almost every company, large or small, every political party, every organization, operates with some kind of overall strategy which helps its members or employees work as a coherent team to achieve the various objectives, goals or aims (these three words are used interchangeably) of that company, political party or organization.

In an advertising agency, which is, after all, just another company, 'the strategy' refers to the strategic plan, also known as the creative brief, devised by the agency for each of its clients' accounts.

That's the strategic plan we'll be talking about in this book – rather than the internal strategic plan which the agency might have for itself as an operating tool for running a better company – although, of course, good agencies would have one of those, too.

WHY DO WE NEED A STRATEGY AND A STRATEGIC PLAN?

However much the landscape of advertising changes, the importance of understanding strategy as you launch into your creative career remains crucial. The penetration of digital media has changed nearly everything. It's changed viewing habits, challenged traditional media, forced brands to react to a crisis within hours, rather than weeks. What hasn't changed is the necessity to understand what motivates a person to do this or that. To choose one thing over another. To stay with one brand, or switch to a new one.

Strategy should underpin all advertising. Sound strategy will ensure that a crisis, such as a product recall, can be managed effectively without the customer losing confidence in the brand.

As an advertising creative, there is an even greater necessity for your message to stand out in this crowded, frenetic, complex communication mix. Moreover, whatever advertising message you do send out, in whichever channel of communication, it's likely to be transformed, in subtle or drastic ways, minute by minute by you and me: the audience. The message, the communication, that you, as a creative person working for a specific client, send out could be altered in unpredictable ways by whoever decides to tweet about that product, place or political issue. In a tweet of 140 characters any of us could help or harm a product or service.

So if it's a constantly changing landscape, you could argue that a clear strategic approach is useless. Why bother? In fact, it's more necessary than ever. In the digital age when consumers are more in control of the message, you need a strong, yet flexible strategy to build a brand that people can trust. One that can withstand a crisis and rebuild that trust if necessary. A brand that people might pay a bit more for, once they go on comparison sites and see that an unknown brand costs only marginally less than the 'famous' one.

A strong, yet flexible strategy can also mean that you avoid producing advertising that's confused, irrelevant to its target market, becomes dated or falls flat. It can help you create advertising that speaks to a global audience, and can communicate on screens as small as your mobile phone, working across all media platforms seamlessly, using each to its best advantage. And, as we'll see exemplified in subsequent chapters, armed with a consistently strong strategy and stand-out creative, even long-established brands can harness digital media with impressive results. The following case study shows how VW launched a car in the digital arena, using an event, social media and a mobile phone game app.

In 2011, Volkswagen celebrated 35 years of their classic Golf GTI with a unique launch event in London of a special-edition anniversary model. A live audience watched as racing driver/TV presenter Amanda Stretton introduced the new car and the GTI's engineers. They raced it through the event space and suddenly it 'vanished' before everyone's eyes, travelling 'back in time', appearing on the screen in front of the startled audience, then on VW's Facebook page (http://www. facebook.com/volkswagenuk) for fans everywhere to follow.

The 'time travel' journey went viral, showing the car first arriving at VW's headquarters at Wolfsburg in 1976, the start of its journey, taking a trip through the decades. It was the first-ever digital launch by a major car manufacturer of a new model.

Accompanying the launch, the GTI Edition 35 app allows you to race the new GTI against the classic 1976 model.

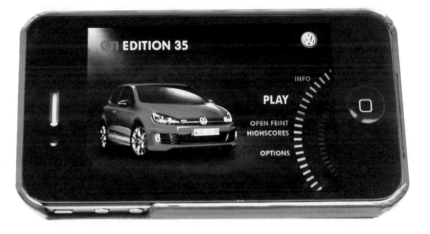

Created for VW by Fishlabs, the award-winning German game developer, this 3-D racing game enables you to select your level of difficulty, and offers a wide choice of options for racing against an opponent in your special-edition GTI. If you want a break from the racing circuit, you can click through to the showroom, or to Volkswagen International, the official Facebook page, where you can 'share your thoughts, pictures and videos of your personal Volkswagen experiences and moments'. All this helps to create brand loyalty while giving fans an enjoyable game.

1   Fans and journalists gather in London at the launch event of the VW Golf GTI Edition 35.

2   The classic 1976 GTI, the relevance of which will soon become apparent.

3   Racing driver and TV presenter Amanda Stretton announces the unveiling.

4   Two engineers take charge and begin driving through the event space towards what appears to be a wall.

5   The car seems to vanish into space, turning into a kind of time machine.

6   The event space is suddenly empty, the car nowhere to be seen or heard.

7   The startled audience strain to see where the engineers have taken the new car!

8   The screen starts to come alive, and in an instant the VW will appear at headquarters, in Wolfsburg, Germany, having travelled back in time.

1	2		4	
	3		5	6
			7	8

A STRONG STRATEGY IS THE KEY

Advertising based on a strong, flexible strategy will always help a brand to stand out and make it sparkle, whatever the medium. The illustrious weekly publication *The Economist* challenged the non-reader to try it.

Consider the ad 'Still or sparkling?'. The award-winning campaign for *The Economist* has always stood out for its clarity, wit and simplicity; for achieving its objective with the minimum of words. This particular ad ran on the inside back cover of the Harden's guide to London restaurants in 2006. It's timeless. It makes you think, 'Yes – I want to be sparkling. In fact, I *must* be sparkling, or I might not get promoted! I had better start reading *The Economist* this week.' David Abbott, writer and one of the founders of London agency Abbott Mead Vickers BBDO, and art director Ron Brown, created this long-running campaign, which launched in 1988 with the now-famous poster: '"I never read The Economist." Management trainee. Aged 42.' The approach looks simple enough in hindsight – but then don't most great ideas?

At the time, it was a risky strategy to begin with this bold, negative statement. It takes you a moment to process the implication: that this person *should* be reading *The Economist*. The tone is both subtle and 'in your face'. Yet it manages to be quick to take in – as a poster has to be. And it didn't alienate existing, loyal readers. After all, if you put off your current market in an attempt to extend it, you could easily be left with no one.

What was the initial insight behind this work? What kind of research led to the strategy that gave this campaign the springboard for such consistent creativity, enabling it to run for a quarter of a century in a changing financial and business world, yet remain fresh, effective, distinctive?

1   The message behind this ad for *The Economist* takes a few seconds to sink in. Seemingly negative in tone, it was a bold, but successful ad that arose out of a larger strategy created by Abbott Mead Vickers BBDO for the publication.

2   This ad for *The Economist* ran on the inside back cover of Harden's 2006 guide to London restaurants. Part of a long-running, wider campaign, the strong strategy ensured that each ad could be written to fit its location while building the brand.

2

Still or sparkling?

The Economist

1

"I never read The Economist."
Management trainee. Aged 42.

UNDERSTANDING STRATEGY HELPS TO SELL YOUR IDEA

Strong strategic thinking lies behind these ads by M&C Saatchi for Dixons, out of which came the award-winning slogan – 'The last place you want to go'.

M&C Saatchi created the memorable campaign line, 'The last place you want to go', for Dixons, a high street retailer of audio-visual technology in the UK. On the face of it the line sounds fairly unpromising. Imagine yourself as the client, hearing that line 'proposed' to you at a meeting. (After all, a proposition is just that – an offer that will in some way benefit you.) Without a creative brief, even an agency with a track record as impressive as M&C Saatchi's would have a devilishly hard time selling it. The strategy, and its resulting proposition, both need the narrative of the whole brief to make it clear to a client why that strategy and that proposition have the potential to lead to convincing, galvanizing creative work.

Get off at the fashionable end of Oxford Street, drift into the achingly cool technology hall of London's most happening department store and view this year's must-have plasma courtesy of the sound and vision technologist in the Marc Jacobs sandals then go to dixons.co.uk and buy it.

Dixons.co.uk
The last place you want to go

Get off at Knightsbridge, visit the discerning shopper's fave department store, ascend the exotic staircase and let Piers in the pinstripe suit demonstrate the magic of the latest high-definition flatscreen then go to dixons.co.uk and buy it.

Dixons.co.uk
The last place you want to go

THE STRATEGIC PLAN OR CREATIVE BRIEF

The creative brief forms the heart of this book, because it is the single most important piece of paper you'll receive in the agency. It can take a variety of forms. You'll see when you begin going on work placements and entering competitions that some creative briefs are extremely short – one line – while others run to a couple of pages. If a product is famous, you'll know more about it, and the brief might not be as complex. But you'll still need to consider the key points – whether you're targeting existing or new consumers, and so on. It's easy to skip a section, but that one section might hold the clue to the others. That's why it's important to consider all of them.

Each agency has a different way of organizing the relevant sections that form their strategic 'plan'. However, the questions that need addressing are the same:

1. Product/Service: What, precisely, is your advertising selling?
2. Objective: What must your advertising achieve?
3. Target Market: Who is the primary focus of your advertising?
4. Strategy: How will your advertising achieve your objective?
5. Proposition: What's the 'hook' that will attract the target market?
6. Support: Why does the product interest this target market?
7. Competition: Who else is fighting for your target market's attention in this area?
8. Mandatory Elements: What has to appear in the advertising – e.g. a legal requirement.
9. Tone of Voice: Describe the campaign's character – in three adjectives, max!
10. Desired Consumer Response: What do you want your target audience to do, feel or think after seeing the advertising?
11. Media Requirement: Where will the advertising appear?

In answering these questions, you will be creating a strategic plan for your advertising. The 11 chapters of this book explore each of these elements one by one to help you build up a basic template for a creative brief.

The planner in an advertising agency has the specific role to write the strategic plan that the client and agency agree to and sign off on. This is what you, the creative team, start working from. A large agency will have several planners. The planner doesn't, or shouldn't, work in isolation. However, ultimately, it's the planner's responsibility to put together the strategic plan, or, to use the agency term, the creative brief. Since it's this document that becomes your starting point, your springboard, it's obviously in your best interest to become part of the planning process from which the creative brief emerges; to understand the process, and to learn how to contribute to it. That's what this book is about.

WHAT IS THE PLANNING PROCESS?

The planning process begins with a meeting between the client and agency, in which the client reveals to the agency the specific problem or issue that they would like the agency to solve or address. If you're in this meeting, pay close attention. It all starts here.

Your agency might be pitching to win new business, with a tight deadline. Or this meeting might be with an existing client about a new product launch. It might be a request, or indeed a demand from the client for a shift of direction for an established product, perhaps because of a sudden change in the market category brought about by, for example, a new competitor or new legislation (e.g. environmental), or perhaps because of a change in brand managers. The person in charge of the brand on the client side might feel the current advertising isn't working hard enough. Maybe he or she just doesn't like it!

RESEARCH

Research is a search for the 'truth'. It underpins every good strategy. The first thing the agency will need to do is learn the truth, as far as it's possible to know it. What is the reality of the situation as it stands for that client's product, the category, and the competition in that category?

A planner, together with the client, will usually commission a considerable amount of research, both qualitative and quantitative. Briefly, these two types of research differ in type and scale. Qualitative (or 'qual') refers to one-to-one consumer interviews, as well as small focus groups, ranging from approximately six to twenty people. Quantitative research means commissioning large studies to gain fresh, relevant data, or buying existing information from large opinion-poll studies. It could include analysing ongoing tracking studies to determine current buying habits. According to its CEO, Ian Cheshire, Kingfisher, the company that owns B&Q (the biggest DIY chain in the world), tracks seven million customers each week to determine their buying habits.

The amount and type of research an agency commissions depends on what they and the client need and can afford, in order to determine what the facts and opinions are about the category, the product, the target market, and the competition. 'There's lots of data,' commented Cheshire on BBC Radio 4's business programme, *The Bottom Line*, 'but not enough insight.' And, in terms of what research can and cannot help you with, Cheshire, in spite of the value he places on research, made the following telling remark: 'You wouldn't have got the iPod out of asking what someone wants.'

So, of course, research is a useful tool but it only goes so far. Exactly how far is a huge topic, controversial to say the least. However, it's safe to say that research will always play some part in forging a strategy, and creating effective, creative advertising.

As a creative person, you should always be doing research. Whether you're working within an agency, or on your portfolio, without anyone else providing information, you and your teammate can accomplish quite a lot of informal research on your own. You'll see in the following chapters how valuable it can be to talk to a friend, a relative, someone older or younger than you, about a problem you're trying to solve about a product or service that's unfamiliar.

You can put together a simple questionnaire and formalize the process. One answer could reveal a 'truth' about that product that you otherwise wouldn't have known. This process can give you the 'emotional response' that might unlock your creativity. Trawling the internet for information produces more data than you can handle. Analysing blogs and Twitter can reveal useful information that was once privileged.

Valuable gems of creative insight can come from research reports. Novelist Fay Weldon began her career as a copywriter at J. Walter Thompson in London in the 1950s. During her time there she created the award-winning, classic 'Go to Work on an Egg' campaign for the Egg Marketing Board. The campaign line sprang nearly word for word from a sentence she was reading in a long, rather dull-looking research document. Many people had read it before her. It summed up the practical benefit of eating an egg for breakfast.

There was memorable TV, and the phrase soon entered the language. The strategic thought – that by eating a protein-rich egg you had the energy to go to work – was clear. At least, it was clear to Fay Weldon!

THE ROLE OF THE CREATIVE IN THE PLANNING PROCESS

Planning should never be a sequential process – a relay race, in which you, the creative person, take the baton only for the last stretch, when it's too late to contribute anything useful and the deadline looms large. There is no doubt that a planner is knowledgeable, can save you time and helps to focus the process of strategic thinking. However, it's a mistake to leave all the initial thinking to your planner.

The more you enjoy the process, and get involved in it, the more chance you have to share your insight, contribute your knowledge, and influence the strategy. We'll touch on that more in the next section. A lively debate about the role of the planner, and how best the planning process should unfold, took place between David Golding and Dave Trott at the IPA (Institute of Practitioners in Advertising) in 2008. In a typically provocative, stimulating entry in his blog following this debate, Rory Sutherland, executive creative director of OgilvyOne, put it simply:

Planning + Creative = Good.
Planning > Creative = Bad.

Rory Sutherland acknowledges that, like most specialists, planners are a good thing, but, he continues, 'our current, sequential approach to using different talents is a dreadful way to use our mix of talents to best effect'. Plenty of people weighed into the argument, saying, in effect, that this sequential approach no longer occurs. That's good news, and even more reason for you to feel that your insight is as valuable as the planner's.

Dave Trott added to the blog following this debate to make it clear how strongly he feels about creative input into strategy: 'I've been teaching creative students for years, and I never give them a brief, just the name of a product. Working out a brief is the first creative thing to learn, media is the second, writing ads is the third. If we assume only planners can write briefs then we have to accept whatever brief we're given. Which is lazy and uncreative. The best people are creative whatever department they're in.'

The planner is outward-facing, just as the account director is: he or she will liaise with the client, as well as with all the members of the internal account team. This team includes the account director, creative director, you, as a member of the creative team, and the media people, who may be part of the agency or a separate company. It's in everyone's interest to achieve the best possible strategic plan – the creative brief – so that you, as part of the creative team, can quickly and creatively address the client's problem.

WHERE DO YOU FIT INTO THE PICTURE?

Overleaf is a diagram which shows you the different departments and individuals who constitute the world of a medium-to-large advertising agency.

This structure varies according to the country you are working in, and whether your agency includes its digital arm within the same space, or whether that is a separate, specialist agency. As part of the creative department, you would show your work to a creative group head, who in turn would present to the creative directors (CDs). The executive creative director then has the final say, in agreement with the managing director (MD) and, of course, the client. Although the lines don't show the planners linking to the creative teams in this diagram, in reality they would be in conversation with you and with your group head and CD. This is merely an indication of the main roles within most agencies.

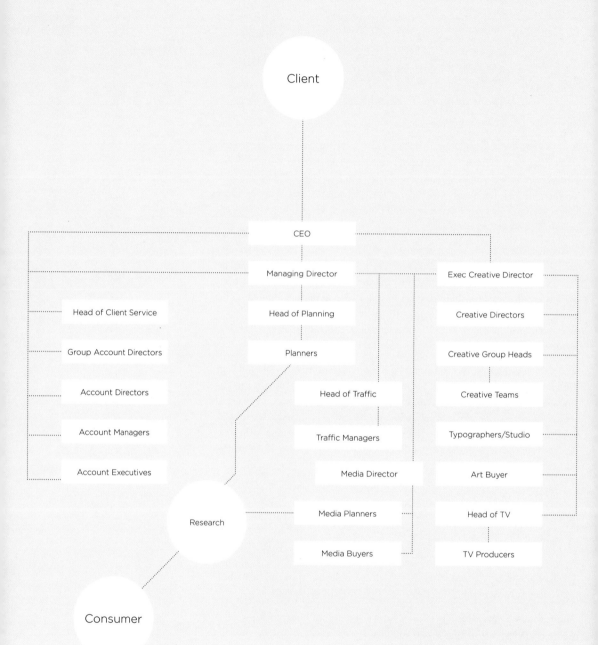

Client

CEO

Managing Director   Exec Creative Director

Head of Client Service   Head of Planning   Creative Directors

Group Account Directors   Planners   Creative Group Heads

Account Directors   Head of Traffic   Creative Teams

Account Managers   Traffic Managers   Typographers/Studio

Account Executives   Media Director   Art Buyer

Research   Media Planners   Head of TV

Media Buyers   TV Producers

Consumer

Diagram courtesy of Rob Kitchen

HOW TO USE THIS BOOK

This book is essentially a workbook, structured around the 11 essential elements of a classic brief – the 11 questions posed earlier – to form the Creative Brief Template. Each element of the brief is assigned its own chapter, each of which explores, unpicks and illustrates the reasoning behind the decisions a planner makes about the aspects of a particular brief from the viewpoint of a creative.

Of course, the architecture, or structure of the brief varies from one agency to another. The template suggested here is designed to be easily adaptable, so that whatever prior learning you have, and in whichever country you're planning to work, you can use it to organize your thoughts quickly, to focus on the key issues: to learn to think strategically.

People are constantly trying to refresh, rephrase, shorten, lengthen this list of categories. This is always happening, but not always to everyone's advantage. If you don't ask all these questions, you might miss the answer that will unlock your creative solution.

Each of these 11 sections goes under many different guises according to the agency. But they all boil down to these basic components. And by using this template, you can quickly translate and make sense of any brief, as well as write your own.

FILLING IN THE CREATIVE BRIEF TEMPLATE

At the end of each chapter you will be invited to fill in the relevant section of the template in relation to a hypothetical brief created for this book – 'Figure 8 Yoghurt'. In analysing the process of formulating the creative brief, chapter by chapter, you'll be able to see what each section of the brief should address. And writing a creative brief yourself is the most effective way of understanding how the process works.

So let's say you're on a placement. Whatever form of creative brief that agency has decided to use, you can always refer to this book as a guide. The various sections of the Creative Brief Template as they are set out in the following chapters represent essential areas that you need to explore in order to solve the problem set by the brief. Problem-solving is really what you're doing when you're creating a campaign. The client comes to an agency with an issue or a problem that needs addressing in some way or another.

By the time you finish this book, you'll be able to write a strong brief. The advertising business is about problem-solving, and what you need to do in order to identify and solve these problems is learn to think strategically. Teaching this skill is the objective of this book. Your ability to solve problems will stand you in good stead throughout your career, even if you change careers!

CASE STUDY:
GALE'S PURE HONEY

Here is a student brief for Gale's Pure Honey devised by Stef Forbes and Fred Wood. It demonstrates how to fill in the Creative Brief Template and shows how a strategy can be created to reflect the target age group. Three of their ads for this campaign follow on. You'll then see the 'Who Are You?' document, which we will discuss in Chapter Three. This can be helpful in figuring out how to 'talk' to the target market. It has been included last, following the creative work, so that you can see how the character Stef and Fred created helped to give them their springboard for the ads.

CREATIVE BRIEF

PRODUCT/SERVICE (What, precisely, is your advertising selling?)
Gale's Pure Honey (Premier Foods)

OBJECTIVE (What must your advertising achieve?)
To encourage children to want to eat Gale's Pure Honey

TARGET MARKET (Who is the primary focus of your advertising?
Primarily, children aged 12–15
Secondarily, parents who are in charge of household purchases

STRATEGY *(How will the advertising achieve its objective?)*
By convincing the 12–15 year old that although he is a bit of a rebel, Gale's Pure Honey can satisfy his sweet tooth

PROPOSITION (What's the 'hook' that will attract the target market? Write it in one clear sentence. This is invaluable as your work-in-progress campaign line – or as your final one)
Gale's Pure Honey. Really sweet (so you don't have to be).

SUPPORT (Why does the product interest this target market? List in order of importance, turning the attributes into benefits wherever possible)

Flexible usage:
• Healthier alternative to sugar (for example, replacing sugar sprinkled on cereal)
• Makes plain foods tastier (bread, cornflakes, milk, etc.)

Squeezy bottle is user friendly:
• Convenient size for hands and cupboards
• Simple to dispense the right amount of the product
• Easy for children to use without making a mess
• Honey crystallizes when in contact with air; the Gale's squeezy

bottle keeps the air out and the honey in, keeping the product fresh
- Use the bottle or honey itself to create pictures/art and crafts in and out of the home

COMPETITION (Who else is fighting for your target market's attention in this area?)
Other honey brands, jam, sugar, etc.

MANDATORY ELEMENTS (What has to appear in the advertising – e.g., a legal requirement?)
The Gale's logo or product shot

TONE OF VOICE (Describe the campaign's character – in three adjectives, max!)
Assured, fun, insightful

DESIRED CONSUMER RESPONSE (What you want your target audience to do, feel or think after seeing the advertising?)
We want children to ask their parents for Gale's Pure Honey on their next shopping trip

MEDIA REQUIREMENT (Where will the advertising appear?)
Three executions: Bus, Traditional Outdoor, Digital Outdoor

WHO ARE YOU?

Describe the person you are talking to. It could be someone you know, or you could create an imaginary character. It has to be someone interested in your propositions. Give this person a good name, so that you have a clear picture in your mind.

Benji Turner, 12 years old

Who he is:
- Lives at home with his mum, dad and little sister Sarah (5)
- Goes to school
- Hobbies: riding his bike, playing football and tag at school. Running around on the playground.
- Favourite subjects: PE and Geography
- Doesn't enjoy homework as he just wants to get out of the house and have fun with his mates

What he likes:
- Swimming
- Football
- Annoying his little sister Sarah
- Playing pranks

What he hates:
- Homework
- Rain
- Bedtime
- Having to tidy his room

Decide what you want to say. What promise or benefit can you offer that you believe will genuinely interest the person you've described. Don't try to be clever at this point. You're not writing copy, just deciding what is your best offer. If you don't have a unique selling point, look for the emotional selling point (see pp. 30 and 167). Write as clearly and briefly as you can, in a conversational tone.

Gale's Pure Honey is a sweet treat. You can enjoy it while still being a naughty little rebel.

Gale's takes care of your sweet tooth, while you can still misbehave.

Imagine precisely how and where the promise or benefit you're presenting connects with the person you're talking to. Where will he or she receive your message as the day unfolds. What mood will this person be in when your message reaches them? You could draw a graph of their day. Now you'll begin to see how the product or service you have to offer fits into that individual's life. Once you understand this, you're ready to write good copy.

Typical weekday

7:00: Benji wakes up and gets ready for school. He has a wash, gets into his school uniform and heads downstairs. He eats his breakfast in front of the TV. *(Mood: tired and can't be bothered to go to school) (Media: TV)*

8:15: Heads to the bus stop where he chats to his mates, while messing around. *(Mood: happy to be around his friends) (Media: bus shelter, bus)*

9:00: School starts. He attends lessons until break time at 11.30. He spends the break playing with his mates and reading a Pokemon magazine with his mates. *(Mood: enjoying his break) (Media: Pokémon magazine)*

11:45: Returns to class until lunch break at 13:15.

13:15: Lunch break. He eats his lunch and then spends the rest of the time chatting to his mates.

14:00: Lessons continue until 15:30.

15:30: School's out. Benji and his mates head into town and walk around the shops. They generally get some pick 'n' mix and just have a laugh. *(Mood: glad school is over and having fun) (Media: billboards)*

17:00: Benji's mum picks him up and he returns home to do some homework.

18:30: Dinner is served. The family sits down together and chats about the day's events.

19:00: Benji will spend the rest of the evening watching TV, finishing off homework, playing computer games, or reading his magazine before heading to bed at 21:00. *(Mood: exhausted from the day) (Media: TV, Pokémon magazine)*

Media that he will come into contact with:
Pokémon magazine
Billboards
Bus shelter, bus
TV

1. PRODUCT/SERVICE:
WHAT, PRECISELY, IS YOUR ADVERTISING SELLING?

This section of the brief relates to the specific product or service to be advertised, as opposed to what the company as a whole is selling. A successful campaign depends on making sure that the product or service being advertised has the potential to attract an audience who will respond in a positive way, and it is the planner's role to examine the product or service itself, as well as the category. There are key questions to ask: some that the client can answer, others that require research. Once the planner distils and analyses the necessary background knowledge, it will start to become clear what kind of

When you launch a product, you can tempt people into trying something new without revealing exactly what it is. However, it might appear as if there is something to hide! In this cartoon, the stall has a name that gives you no idea of the product on sale. So unless the smell is tantalizing, the stallholder is unlikely to have many customers.

communication can solve the client's problem. Other areas apart from advertising, to do with how the product or service is marketed, might also need attention to increase the brand's success. This should form part of your research and discussion with the client.

Advertising isn't always the solution to a client's problem. Leslie Butterfield, Interbrand's chief strategy officer and former planning director of London agency Butterfield Day Devito Hockney, believes that 'as a strategist, your perspective has to be broader than this to gain the client's confidence … [you need to] interrogate the product, and take a long hard look at all those other aspects of the marketing mix that just might do the job better than a 30-second commercial.'

BACKGROUND RESEARCH

The process of analysing the product or service starts with research. If this is a new client, or a new business pitch, it's vital to understand the product or service in depth. Is it new? What gap, if any, does it fill in the market? How well does it perform against competitors? The agency will want to know what advertising has and hasn't worked for the company in the past. Equally important is to hear the client's opinion on why. Was it to do with the product featured in the campaign? Or how that product was advertised? Perhaps the advertising was aimed at the wrong audience. It could have been the right audience but at the wrong time of year.

Only by analysing the answers to these and many other questions specific to each product or service can the agency gain insight into the client's problem and decide whether, and how, advertising can solve it. Isolating the individual product or service to be advertised, especially when dealing with corporate multinational clients, such as IBM, is the first step towards relevant, effective, creative advertising.

INTERROGATE THE PRODUCT

Good advertising depends on examining the product closely. What does it do, and how does its performance relate to the consumer? Consider the stylish ads for the Italian company Stella on the following pages, whose coffee maker is one of their many sleek, stainless steel homewares. How does its performance relate to the coffee-drinking consumer? It results in good, strong coffee. By interrogating the product – asking what it does – and identifying that the intense flavour of strong coffee is what consumers desire from their coffee maker, the agency arrived at a strategic solution to capture the consumer's attention with images of intense sensation, which enabled them to make the creative leap to this campaign. The advertising answers the client's stated mission, which is to promote the 'intense moments even in simple everyday gestures'.

Shirts can pick a tie for you.

IBM helped a German retailer boost customer satisfaction 18% with dressing rooms that actually suggest accessories. Want smarter retail? ibm.com/smarterplanet

 IBM

The intensity, or 'bite', of the coffee that you make with the product appeals to consumers. This is symbolized in the advertisement in the bite of the coffee-bean spider.

Although the size of the product, the coffee maker, is small in relation to the lips, its impact is huge because of the focus on the coffee's bite.

WHO CONDUCTS THE RESEARCH?

Planners are mainly responsible for gathering and distilling the research. They will buy in existing research where appropriate, and, depending on the time frame, commission new research, often in the form of focus groups, to gain specific insight into how consumers feel about a particular product or service. Sifting and analysing all that information requires skill. If a client doesn't have a marketing department, the agency's account-handling department joins the planner. Thus, the agency takes on a larger role.

VISITING 'THE FACTORY'

Visiting 'the factory' – a generic term for a client's base of operations – can be the most rewarding of all research activities. If you're with an agency, the account handler or planner will probably accompany you. Whether you're working in an agency, or as a freelance, try to visit early on in your research.

The 'factory' might be a farm, bank, dairy, hospital, supermarket, museum, or, of course, an actual factory. The point is that you will have the chance to witness first hand the process of people creating the product, or delivering the service, to be advertised. Take notes – and photos, if possible – and speak with the people who spend all day involved in the process. They're usually proud of their work. Listen to their views. You'll come away with a deeper understanding of what your advertising is selling. Your curiosity and enthusiasm during the visit will encourage people to talk to you. The knowledge you come away with will give your advertising the stamp of authority, and increase your confidence as you work on the campaign. You can usually contact a specific person to ask further questions if you need to.

RESEARCHING ON YOUR OWN

If you're working in a small agency without a planner, or if you're freelance, you will need to rely on your own research skills, as well as on the client, to provide

information. Visiting the factory is only the beginning. The client's knowledge is invaluable, but it can be limited or one-sided, particularly in terms of the competition, so you will always need to look further. Thanks to the internet, more information than ever is available if you know where to find it. Social networking sites provide a range of opinions, useful when you're working in product categories unfamiliar to you, outside your own age-range and interest. Equally, if it's something you know about and use, objectivity is sometimes difficult. Hearing other people's opinions, whether positive or negative, is vital.

KEY QUESTIONS

There are several key questions that need answering as part of the research process undertaken by the planner, or by you, if you're working freelance or for a small agency.

WHY DO YOU BUY THIS BRAND? (OR WHY DON'T YOU?)

As you know from your own life, a consumer's relationship with a brand is unique, and changes over time. No product or service is ever perfect, so there is always room for improvement.

When planners analyse the relevant trends in a category, they begin to identify opportunities and flag up potential problems, all of which forms a basis for understanding the client's problem. A skilled planner soon develops a line of thinking, a hypothesis, that further research (e.g. focus groups or one-to-one interviews) may confirm or confound. Either way, it will provide valuable guidance on how best to proceed. This qualitative research is particularly useful in helping the agency to understand how a consumer relates to that product or brand.

IS THERE A USP? WHAT IS THE ESP?

A unique selling point (USP) is what makes a product distinctive. When a product establishes a new category, there is a clear USP at launch stage. Of course, this doesn't always last very long. Depending on the category, months or years later, competitors will have blurred, or eradicated, the original product's distinctiveness. That makes it harder to advertise the superiority of a product, and hard for consumers to choose the best-performing product in the category.

However, a product can still be successful even without a USP, if it has an ESP: an emotional selling point. Agency and client need to 'engage the consumer' with a conversation appropriate to the product and its audience. If we like the way the brand 'talks' to us, assuming we're satisfied with the product's performance, we are less likely to switch to a competitor. Engaging the consumer is vital in a crowded category. We might flirt with other brands, and then return to the original. So we need to look for an ESP.

Pepto-Bismol's conversation with their customers is clear and empathetic. The product's original formula, a thick pink liquid, was invented by a doctor in 1901 to treat infant diarrhoea. It continues to be a leading, trusted remedy for adult heartburn, indigestion, upset stomach and diarrhoea. Many competitors have since entered the market, but the 'pink stuff', as it's been called in various campaigns, is the original. That's its USP. Pepto-Bismol's advertising reflects an understanding of the need for an ESP as well, to engage the consumer. In addition, Pepto-Bismol comes in tablets – keeping up with the competition means offering new, more convenient forms of an established product.

In its Spanish-language TV commercial (opposite), a hot and spicy empanada, a food almost guaranteed to cause an upset stomach, does the talking – and drives the car! – while breaking up with its girlfriend. The campaign line advises the sufferer: 'Don't let the food you love hurt you.'

PERCEIVED PRODUCT DIFFERENCE

A perceived USP can achieve as much as a genuine USP or an ESP. How you position the product within the wider category can achieve this effect. As an alkaline battery, Duracell has a clear advantage over non-alkaline, zinc carbon batteries. It lasts up to five times longer. By making the strategic decision to compete against 'ordinary' zinc carbon batteries (as opposed to other alkalines lasting the same length of time as a Duracell), the agency could advertise this consumer benefit. It became Duracell's USP, which any other alkaline could have used. It was a perceived USP against other alkaline batteries.

Since zinc carbon batteries were far cheaper than alkaline ones, they were bought more often. Research showed that consumers had little interest in learning the

1–2   'Empanada', this wonderfully melodramatic US Spanish-language TV commercial for Pepto-Bismol, shows how a product can endear itself to its audience. The actual product Pepto-Bismol is so well known there's no need to explain how it works.

3   'It's over.'

4   'Why??'

5   'It was all a lie ... I'm now going out with your sister. Get out of the car.'

8   'Don't let the food you love hurt you.'

1   2
3   4
5   6
7   8

CAN YOU REMEMBER THE LAST TIME THEY CHANGED ITS BATTERIES?

1

1   This poster allying the Duracell battery that goes on and on to Big Ben, a symbol of reliability and longevity, was part of an award-winning UK advertising campaign. It followed the successful Bunnies TV advertising, carrying the principle of the long-lasting battery into other media.

2   The surreal notion of a bus running on Duracell adds humour to the campaign, while extending the media choices.

2

Translation: 'Even more power to last longer.'

In France and Italy, the launch of the even longer-lasting battery, Ultra, was advertised using the concept of fusion created by thousands of bunnies powered by batteries melding into one giant creative power.

difference between alkaline and zinc carbon. There had to be a very good reason to buy the more expensive option. Convenience. While people are hungry for information about a major purchase that is visible, a source of pleasure, often a status symbol (a new car, for example), batteries are a low-interest product, within the category of 'repeat' purchase items, referred to as a 'negative purchase'. When the item runs out you have to replace it (like toilet paper). The fewer times you have to replace them, the better.

Dancer Fitzgerald Sample, Duracell's US agency, translated the uniqueness of Duracell against zinc carbon batteries into this single-minded promise: you won't have to replace Duracell as often as 'ordinary' batteries. In 1973, they launched the Duracell bunny, the toy that just goes on and on working long after other battery-powered toys have fallen by the wayside. It has since gone global, becoming one of advertising's most memorable images. The visualization of the Duracell bunny changes according to regional differences and the fashion of the times.

Having implanted the concept of the battery that goes on and on in the public consciousness through the memorable 'Bunnies' TV ad, Duracell then used the concept in other forms of advertising. In the UK, taking on larger-than-life objects, like the iconic Big Ben, and applying the concept of the long-lasting performance gave the Duracell product personality and visibility. Posters proved successful, creating awareness and building the brand alongside TV.

IS THE PRODUCT OR SERVICE NEW?

Few aspects of advertising are more exciting than launching a new product. If you get the opportunity to be part of a product's initial development, you can use your creativity to shape its character and give it a unique personality. You will feel a genuine affinity with the brand.

Richard Reed, co-founder of the Innocent smoothie brand, worked in advertising for four years prior to setting up the business. Reed's experience no doubt helped him to understand the importance of a great name and how it determines the concept of the product. 'Innocent' tells the consumer there are no additives in this product, nothing to hide, and that is the message behind the brand. Although Reed didn't develop the product at the agency, it's a great example of strategic thinking and creativity from product origination onward.

Reed and his partners spent six months working on recipes in their kitchen, and then branched out to test them on a wider audience from a stall at a music festival. The response was so positive they gave up the day job and started what is now the number one smoothie brand in the UK – going from zero to £100 million since 1998. Innocent is sold all over Europe.

The 'Innocent' name and the
simple graphics give the product
a fresh, honest image and an ESP.

1

2

HOW DIFFERENT IS THE BRAND EXTENSION?

A strong brand can be successfully extended into new product categories. Sometimes, the extension is in a totally different category from the original, but if the consumer base for both is largely the same, it can work very well. For example, major supermarket brands now extend into the financial sector, including offerings of banking, credit cards, as well as home, car and pet insurance.

Many brand extensions involve introducing products similar to the original, yet with enough of a difference to attract a new, and potentially much larger, audience.

A good example of this is smoothie-maker Innocent's entry into the vast fruit juice market. As a result of its familiarity as a smoothie, the brand now benefits from far more shelf space than other new entries, and offers consumers an ever-widening choice, continuing its conversation of pure ingredients, and its 'halo' graphics.

IS THE CLIENT ASKING YOU TO ADVERTISE A SINGLE PRODUCT OR THE BRAND?

Consumers have a lot on their minds. Advertising more than one product at a time in any particular piece of communication is rarely effective or creative. The client is often keen to do this, since it appears to save money – one ad doing many things. However, the agency needs to help the client understand that this creates a diffused, less successful ad.

Charity advertising, as well as corporate, and retail, all pose huge challenges to the agency of how to crystallize what the audience needs to learn from the advertising, and what they can subsequently follow up on via a website.

1   Technological breakthrough products are exciting and often complex, but you have to understand how they work to write an informative website. GE needed to advertise their re-charging stations for electric cars. This ad makes the charging station look as simple to use as a parking meter.

The copy reads: 'The WattStation™ from GE 2011 CES Award Winner for Best Innovation. It seems like we've been waiting a long time for the electric car, but maybe the electric car was waiting for this, The WattStation™ is an easy-to-use electric vehicle charger. It's changing the way we get to where we all want to go. Learn more about the electric vehicle charging station at ecomagination.com/wattstation.'

2   When new entries from successful brands launch into established markets, such as smoothie-maker Innocent's move into the fruit juice market, a familiar name and product imagery appeals to the brand's established consumer base, as well as attracting new fans.

IS YOUR WORRYING
GLOBAL ENOUGH?

FACE THE PROBLEM BEFORE IT'S TOO LATE.

LEGAMBIENTE

GREY

3

When you have a huge chain of stores selling thousands of individual products, which can't be advertised all at once, the brand is the product. Supermarkets are an example of this challenging problem.

Also, do-it-yourself (DIY) stores. An award-winning example of how this plays out in advertising is 'The Hymn of Doing' (see overleaf), a refreshingly creative 2009 German TV commercial for Hornbach, a leading German chain of DIY stores. The commercial suggests you should go about and look at what you want to achieve, the projects you want to undertake, with the underlying message that this DIY store understands your wildest dreams and can help you achieve some of them.

3   Legambiente, a major Italian environmental organization, brings into focus the complex, vital issues facing us, with this stark, human approach. Advertising everything they do would be impossible, so the distilled message highlights a common human tendency to worry about a small wrinkle, ignoring global problems – represented here by the fractured head.

In German, the copy rhymes, accompanying surprising and prosaic images, celebrating the dream, the mess, the freedom and joy of 'doing'. Very occasionally a product (paint, watering can, rose) appears.

1   'The wonky table. The old demolition. Make it into your project.'

2   'The creaking stairs. The lost bets.'

3   'The lacking funds.'

4   'The titles won.'

5   'The bench. The bankrupt.'

6   'The sea. The cliché. Make it into your project.'

7   'The dream. The forgotten dream.'

8   'The fantastic dream. The reality.'

9   'The other reality. The absurdity. Make it into your project.'

10   'What you had to do. What you ought to do. What you might be able to do.'

11   'Bureaucracy. Democracy. Biology. Zoology.

     Make it into your project.
     The kohlrabi. The coal tit.

     The little/The large.

     The can. The rose. The broken (object).

     Make it into your project.'

12   The nothing. The everything.
     The beginning. The end.

     Make it into your project.'

     Hornbach: There is always something to do. hornbach.de

PRODUCTS HAVE TO ADAPT

Clients sometimes assume that because their product or service appealed to one generation, it will naturally appeal to the next, without any change or updating to suit their needs or desires. A client with a successful product is especially likely to believe that making any change to it is pointless and even frivolous. Often it's the agency's role to convince the client that adapting the product to a new generation is essential for its survival. It's important to distinguish what's good about a product and what needs changing. To maintain their success, classic products, especially in the luxury sector of the market – for example, watches or cars – all have to keep innovating to attract savvy consumers, while retaining key aspects of their brand heritage.

IS THE PRODUCT OR SERVICE BEING REVIVED?

An agency and its client have to know how to use the brand's history in order to re-launch a product successfully. Before you decide which elements to include in the advertising, you need to establish whether the product as it stands can be revived. Advertising alone might not be the whole answer. The agency has to consider these wider trends: political, economic, societal, technological, environmental, legal – whatever is relevant to that category, to make the newly revived product suit the demands of the current market.

In his excellent book *Strategy in Practice*, George Tovstiga, Professor of Strategy and Innovation Management at Henley Business School, writes: 'Determinants of past success are all too often assumed to hold invariably for the future.' Tovstiga cites examples in the car industry, a business sector that seems particularly apt to make drastic assumptions.

He harks back to Henry Ford's well-known remark in 1922: '… any customer can have a car painted in any colour that he wants, as long as it is black'.

But the much-loved Model-T Ford was under threat. Its success blinded Henry Ford to what was happening in America. His inability, or refusal, to see that different styles and colours had already begun to tempt the public meant that he resisted change, sticking to basic black, bringing the Ford Motor Company, by 1945, to near-bankruptcy.

Tovstiga believes: 'Strategic questions, when they arise, are inevitably triggered by changing conditions. Most often these will be externally driven.' The acronym PESTEL is a helpful tool to remind you of six aspects mentioned earlier, against which you can monitor a product's viability: political, economic, societal, technological, environmental and legal.

These aspects aren't abstract notions – they define our everyday world.

When you realize the impact of any one of these six aspects on a consumer's mood, and on their propensity to buy a particular product, you begin to realize

The original Mini was launched in 1959 and became a cult car. BMW launched the first 'new generation' Mini in 2001 and the challenge to the creatives was to use the original Mini heritage and update it for the twenty-first century. Here they offer an escape, whatever the weather, in a convertible updated for contemporary consumers with in-car social media.

TODAY'S
WEATHER
REPORT.
WHATEVER.

MINI Convertible. Come rain or shine our drivers are always looking to find an excuse to go for another spin. With our new in-car social media technology (Facebook, Twitter, web radio) we may have just found that excuse. Test drive a Convertible today at your nearest MINI dealer. **MINI.co.uk**

CASE STUDY:

SHAPE 'N' FRY

A long-standing client proposed a new way to make chips in response to a competitor, which had successfully launched frozen chips. Research showed that this breakthrough convenience product was gradually replacing home made. Since there were always potatoes in the house, home made and frozen co-existed, served on different occasions. Both were strong competition for this proposed entry. Home-made chips made from real potatoes were the 'gold standard'. They took time to scrub, peel, cut and fry, but they were delicious. A family 'treat', and cheap.

Just add water

The new product looked simple – potato powder in a foil pouch. Add the right amount of water to turn it into dough, then shape into a large pancake. Slice into strips – not too thin or they fall apart. Lift the strips with a spatula, slide them into a frying pan, turn gently, lift them out. No one on the agency team managed to make a batch of these chips without breaking them. Their children refused to eat 'broken chips'. Even the home economist ran into problems. The dough's consistency was tricky to get right. The agency advised the client not to launch the product in its present form. The client asked the agency to reserve judgement until the research came in.

The voice of the consumer

The creative team named the product Shape 'n' Fry and mocked up appetizing visuals for the foil pouches. These were sent to women to try the product at home, prior to attending focus sessions. The agency team and client sat behind a two-way mirror listening to comments: 'If I were going to all that trouble, I'd make "real" chips – from potatoes.' Others said the frozen variety had won them over. Shape 'n' Fry 'wasn't real or convenient'. One woman made a supreme effort to sound positive: 'Say there was a thunderstorm, the car had broken down, the children were hungry, and I had no potatoes left. Then I *might* make it.' Behind the mirror, the client smiled with relief. The woman paused. 'No,' she sighed, 'I'd give them cereal.'

Advertising can also kill a product

The client insisted on going ahead. The creative team made a TV commercial which ran in a test market. The product sank like, well, a sack of potatoes. Consumers, attracted by the advertising, tried it once, and never again. They told their friends not to bother. The product was dropped. Why was it made? Because the client could. They had the manufacturing capability from similar ingredients within their brand. But Shape 'n' Fry neither answered the consumer's demand for convenience, nor could it replace their desire for delicious home-made chips.

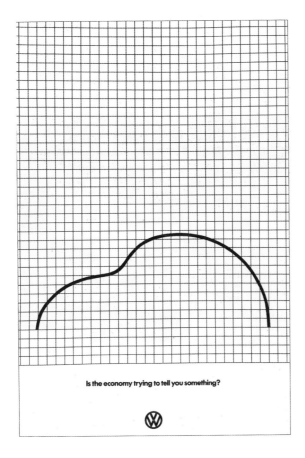

Is the economy trying to tell you something?

how important it is for both your client and the agency, to pay attention to these external factors.

Mirroring Henry Ford's approach in the first half of the twentieth century, many brands producing gas-guzzling cars in the US in the second half of the century failed to recognize that oil prices would rise and assumed that everything would remain the same and they could continue to produce the same machines. But brands like VW and Toyota with smaller, less fuel-thirsty cars stole the march on the established US marques. Whenever the economy took a dip, or petrol prices rose, VW reminded the American public to 'think small', a phrase coined by Bill Bernbach, founder of Doyle Dane Bernbach (DDB). This phrase chimed with what was going on. It showed that VW and DDB understood the changing economic climate, as well as the mood of the individual consumer within it. DDB successfully engaged the consumer's attention and showed how and why VW cars were relevant to their lives.

PRODUCTS MUST ANSWER A CONSUMER NEED OR DESIRE

It's never easy to challenge the client when the product doesn't seem right. Like any relationship, a good client/agency partnership depends on a frank exchange of views. You should feel empowered in an agency to comment, to be honest and helpful, because if you create a whole run of ads that fail because the product is not good, you will lose the client anyway.

In their message to consumers that VW cars were more economical, DDB produced a graph showing the downturn of the economy. The graph is, of course, in the shape of VW's classic 'Beetle'. The car had become so recognizable a few years following its launch, a line drawing was enough.

This witty Italian VW commercial is product-focused. It fulfils Bernbach's vision of VW as honest, simple, reliable, sensible, different, though the Passat is far more luxurious than the Beetle! The driver enjoys the journey, but is then brought back to reality when he arrives home and is accidentally sprayed with water through his open window from a hosepipe wielded by the gardener.

KEEP THE PRODUCT IN FOCUS

If you keep the product in focus and relate its benefits to how the consumer views that product, you're far more likely to create effective advertising. Bernbach saw the VW as 'honest, simple, reliable, sensible, different. And he wanted the advertising to be that way too,' according to his long-time partner, Bob Levenson. As a global brand, VW communicates within different political, economic, societal, technological, environmental and legal conditions. Yet it retains its essential brand characteristics.

'The product. The product. Stay with the product,' said Bernbach. Product-focused advertising is VW's trademark and it continues to steer their distinctive, award-winning creative work in global markets.

START TO DEVELOP YOUR CREATIVE BRIEF FOR FIGURE 8 YOGHURT

In this exercise we are imagining the issues and solutions surrounding a hypothetical food and dairy client whose yoghurt brand is called Figure 8.

Background: The client wants the agency to advertise their low-fat yoghurt range. They have several low-fat ranges. Which one do they want to advertise? Which one should they advertise? It depends on the problem they want to solve. They tell the agency they need to widen their market to include more men, yet their product aimed at men doesn't seem to be attracting them. Figure 8, aimed at women, and doing really well, has the same flavours as the one aimed at men.

The agency conducts focus research groups. These reveal that the men are 'borrowing' Figure 8 from their girlfriend or wife, but not buying it for themselves. When the men are on their own (if they're not in a living-together relationship, and have a separate flat), they are far less likely to buy Figure 8, even though they would like to eat it. They don't bother buying any yoghurt. Figure 8 is seen as too 'girly'. And they aren't buying the product that's aimed at them.

So should the packaging change? Should there be separate websites for men and women? Is there a way to leave the product as it is, and solve this with advertising in another way?

In the first section of your brief, write Figure 8 low-fat yoghurt.

In our hypothetical brief, we're deciding that the client and agency have agreed that Figure 8 is the product that's going to be advertised. In the next chapter we set the objective.

An objective sets out the goal, or aim, of your advertising. It identifies the end result of the process, defining advertising's specific role in solving the problem set by the client. However small or large the budget, whatever the media, an objective answers the basic, key question: 'What must your advertising achieve?'

We live in goal-oriented societies so it's not surprising that the term 'objective' is so familiar. From politics to business, sport to education, everyone has an objective. The politician aims to win the next election. A sports figure sets out to better his or her performance. A company manager's objective is to improve the balance sheet. A charity sets a goal to raise funds for a particular cause. You have your own, personal objectives, or goals.

Whatever the strategy, whatever the executions, keep asking yourself as you develop your work: 'Does it meet the objective?' It's what you will be asked by your creative director and, subsequently, by your client. Whether or not people *like* your creative work is a separate discussion that can only follow if the work meets the objective. It's important that you understand it. How you define and write the objective influences the strategy and your creative work.

Fighting for great creative work, such as this Brazilian ad created by Giovanni + Draft FCB within the global Fiat van campaign, is much easier once you establish that your advertising meets the agreed objective. Here, the objective is to encourage someone running an expanding small business, in this case a fishmonger, to upgrade to Fiat's larger van – *'Pensando em trocar de van?'* ('Thinking of changing your van?').

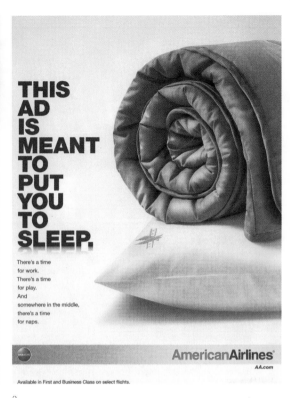

1   2

HOW DO YOU ARRIVE AT THE OBJECTIVE?

1   See if you can define a precise objective for this ad in one sentence.

2   Time is precious, so offering passengers the power to control it is an appealing and persuasive objective, which these ads from American Airlines achieve by emphasizing the on-board facilities offered by the airline.

Whether you're talking about an advertising objective or a personal aim, the question is: what are you trying to achieve? If you were the planner, how would you have written the objective for the American Airlines ad above? It's clear and striking, announcing that a new feature, the 'powerport', is available to First and Business Class passengers, and to 'selected rows' in Economy. We don't have access to the creative brief, so the following three examples are hypothetical. (It's a useful exercise to take an existing ad and work backwards. Imagine the possible objectives. Analyse their strengths and weaknesses. You can continue to do this on your own.)

The following three suggestions home in with increasing insight and accuracy on the true objective behind this finished American Airlines ad.

1. To sell more seats in First and Business Class, and some in Economy

It's not much help to a creative team to receive a brief with an objective so general it could apply to any airline, any new feature. The job of a good planner is to provide the creative team with information as well as insight into what that information means in relation to the client's problem. In this instance, a planner would need to know what the competitive airlines are offering. Are leisure travellers filling the more expensive seats rather than business travellers, now that companies are feeling the pinch and cutting back on upgrades for their employees? Is loyalty to an airline at risk because of other reasons, perhaps a change in destination routes? What do focus groups reveal about the in-flight features passengers currently demand, or desire, from their airline?

The planner analyses the research and – this is the hard part – distils it into one clear sentence: an objective that is neither too general, providing insufficient direction and insight, nor too narrow, allowing for little creative freedom.

2. To announce to First and Business Class travellers that American Airlines offers powerports

It's straightforward and announces the new feature. This objective starts to define the direction for the rest of the brief, and reinforces the campaign line that underpins their current advertising: 'We know why you fly.' The target is more focused. We will look at target audience in the next chapter, but for now, note that if only a few rows of Economy have this feature, the main thrust of the objective should be addressed to First and Business Class.

This second example is clear but does it offer any insight? Does it speak to the consumer, or just announce the feature? What would steer the creative brief into an area which could provide the greatest potential for relevant, creative executions such as this one? Think about what this feature offers to these passengers. The clue is in the copy: control. Powerports offer them the choice of working, resting, choosing their entertainment from their own laptop, at their seat. However simple, the objective must be relevant to the needs or desires of the primary target market. This relevance begins, of course, with the product or feature itself. And the way in which the objective is written should reflect this relevance. The objective has to 'speak' to these travellers.

3. To announce to First and Business Class passengers that flying with American Airlines enables you to control your time

An objective written in this way would give you, the creative team, the insight that you need. It offers to First and Business Class the ability 'to control your time'. This is a distinctive, desirable aim for your advertising to achieve. The objective would spark your creativity. If American Airlines were the first to develop this feature, an objective written in the above way might inspire you to originate the name 'powerport'. Power is a concept you can work with creatively, using it, for example, in the headline and copy. 'Powerport' transforms a useful, practical, relevant technological feature into a desired consumer benefit, and turns it into a bigger idea. Even if other airlines offer these ports, using 'power' in the headline and copy helps to brand the powerport feature as a unique benefit of flying with American Airlines.

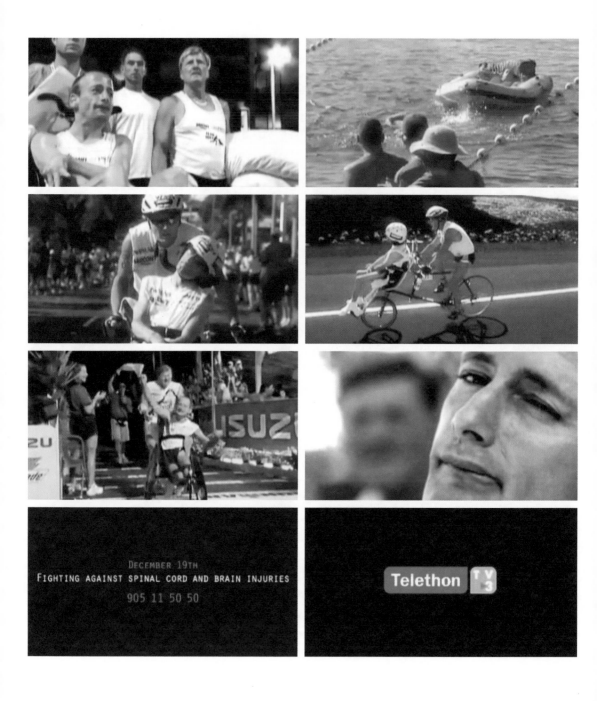

A GOOD OBJECTIVE REQUIRES INSIGHT

Information is only one part of what's required to write a good objective. Insight is required at this stage, as it is throughout the creative brief process. What is insight? It's the ability to perceive something clearly, or deeply. And from that perception, you often understand quite suddenly the nature of a problem, or how a person truly feels about something.

David Abbott, celebrated writer and founder of Abbott Mead Vickers believes: 'The greatest ideas are those which contain a human insight – an insight into human behaviour, for example, with which a reader can relate.'

Consider this example. Raising money for charities is a huge challenge. You might think that the objective would be written in the same way for every charity: 'to raise funds'. That would be far too general. As general as the first of the three previous examples for American Airlines: 'to sell more seats'.

Now consider the objective for the award-winning Spanish commercial 'Team Hoyt', for the Spinal Cord and Brain Injury Telethon: 'to convince viewers about the importance of their donations in fighting against spinal cord and brain injuries'.

Writing the objective in this way shows an insight into what could motivate a viewer to donate money to this cause. The strategy stemming from this objective resulted in a strong creative brief. This, in turn, led to a creative leap to this excellent commercial.

The TV commercial celebrates the courage of Rick Hoyt and his father Dick, both determined to challenge the spinal cord and brain injuries that Rick suffers from, a fight that the charity supports.

It follows the extraordinary true story of Rick Hoyt and his father, who as a family team have participated in over 900 endurance tests and six 'Ironman' triathlons (swimming, cycling and running events). After their first race Rick said, 'Dad, when I'm running, it feels like I'm not handicapped.'

The award-winning Spanish commercial 'Team Hoyt' uses a documentary style of filming to convey its message. There is no dialogue, only the music and lyrics from Simon and Garfunkel's 'Bridge Over Troubled Water'.

SETTING A WINNING OBJECTIVE

John Hegarty, founding partner and Worldwide Creative Director of Bartle Bogle Hegarty (BBH), built his agency on the belief that new business should be won

'Team Hoyt' (opposite) was created by advertising agency Bassat Ogilvy, Barcelona, Spain. The commercial is over two minutes long, and won a Silver Lion at the 2011 Cannes Lions International Festival of Creativity.

Depicting the Hoyts' true story convinces viewers that the charity is worth supporting, without overtly asking for money, nor stating how much the charity needs.

on the strength of the agency's strategic thinking. Consequently, no creative work was ever shown at the pitch stage. This radical departure set BBH apart, and sent a message to prospective clients that defining the overall strategy for a brand was paramount to the success of any advertising effort. It also gave their creative work an even higher premium.

TO CONVINCE LEVI STRAUSS TO RETURN TO THEIR ROOTS

The underlying objective that won BBH the pitch to global client Levi Strauss was to rebuild the brand values, a huge task that was acknowledged to be one of the strengths of the finished advertising. At the new business pitch, BBH took the brave position to tell the client 'the unvarnished truth'. As Hegarty recalled: 'The solution to their deeply troubled brand lay within them. They had to have confidence in who they were, where they'd come from and what they stood for.'

Hegarty was not suggesting a stuck-in-the-past approach. 'They should not apologize for who they were, but celebrate it in a way that was relevant. ... The future for Levi Strauss was in rebuilding the brand's values by reigniting youth's love of their product.'

ADVERTISING'S ROLE IN DEVELOPING A BRAND'S IMAGE

'The Role of Advertising in Brand Image Development', the title of an article by University College Dublin's Professor of Marketing, Tony Meenaghan, explores advertising's capability in this area: 'Advertising has a central role to play in developing brand image, whether at the corporate, retail or product level. It informs consumers of the functional capabilities of the brand while simultaneously imbuing the brand with symbolic values and meanings relevant to the consumer.'

Without taking the first step – convincing Levi Strauss to return to its roots as a

While the specific objective of this groundbreaking ad was, as Hegarty explains, to capitalize on the fashionability of Levi Strauss, it was the underlying objective which won them this global account. Not only is the black sheep a different colour, it is also going in the opposite direction to the crowd, representing a new departure for Levi Strauss – black jeans. Having taken the jeans manufacturer back to its blue denim roots, the ad could then take the company in a new direction.

producer of denim jeans – BBH would not have won the account and could never have achieved the successful, memorable creative work, of which this ad was the beginning. Beautifully art-directed by Hegarty, with the great campaign line written by Barbara Nokes – 'when the world zigs, zag' – it encapsulates the strategic thinking in which BBH excels. The black sheep became BBH's logo. How did BBH achieve the rebuilding of those brand values? We'll look at that in the chapter on strategy. Opposite is the artwork from the now-famous ad, BBH's first, which, in 1982, launched black denim jeans for the American client Levi Strauss.

If one of your personal objectives were to stop smoking, this searing Brazilian ad could convince you to make it a short-term, rather than long-term, goal. The campaign line reads 'Stop Consuming Your Body'.

HOW TO WRITE AN OBJECTIVE

The way in which you write an objective helps to define the difference between the 'what' and the 'how': between the objective (what the advertising must achieve) and the strategy (how to achieve it). Here are two useful tips:

Begin with the word 'to'. You probably noticed that the examples so far all begin with an infinitive ('to do something').

To announce to First and Business Class passengers that flying with American Airlines enables you to control your time. To convince Levi Strauss to return to their roots. To rebuild brand values.

This sentence structure makes it easier to write a clear objective.

Don't use the word 'and'. This will ensure that you keep each objective separate, one per brief. It will help you spot the difference between a sharply focused objective and one that's vague, or masquerading as two objectives. Unsuccessful advertising often stems from an imprecise objective, or from trying to achieve more than one aim at a time.

AS AN EXERCISE, WRITE DOWN FOUR PERSONAL OBJECTIVES

Think of long- and short-term objectives. For example, 'to achieve my personal best in next week's match' (short-term) versus, 'to save for a trip I'm planning to take a year from now' (long-term). Even if your agency has planners, knowing how to write clear objectives will enable you to take part in the process of shaping the brief. Knowing how to write an objective is essential when you're putting together your portfolio, and later on, if you're working in an agency without planners or in a freelance capacity, when you're speaking directly with clients.

Once you've written down your objectives, reflect on how you arrived at them. Were they goals that you've had in mind for a long time? What aspects of your life did you have to consider? Make a note of your thoughts next to each objective. At this point, you're not deciding *how* to achieve these objectives – that's the job of the strategy. If an objective is incredibly ambitious, it will have an immediate impact on how it can be achieved – on the strategy.

Imagine that your friend has set this objective: 'To join next year's Olympic swimming team'. Let's suppose that your friend has only ever competed in local swim meets. And although he or she has done really well, there is less than a month to train. Realistically, no strategy will work. Now imagine this is your client. How would you advise him or her? You can see the dilemma.

MAKE SURE IT'S A SMART OBJECTIVE

You've probably come across the acronym 'SMART'. The letters stand for **S**pecific, **M**easurable, **A**ttainable, **R**elevant, **T**ime-bound. These five words are used to set objectives. It's a helpful tool to use, especially when working freelance, as a checklist to help you set ambitious, yet achievable objectives. An agency planner is responsible for this, but as a creative person whose work will be measured against the objective, you have a stake in this process.

An objective can, and should be, ambitious. You'd like to encourage your friend – or, in the case of advertising, your client. At the same time, an objective must be attainable within the given time, budget and capability of the person, product or service.

HOW TO QUESTION THE OBJECTIVE WHEN IT'S NOT SMART

It's hard, especially when you're starting out, to question the brief, but your opinion is valuable.

John Hegarty gives this advice: 'Never just blindly accept the brief. Challenge it, interrogate it, question its very foundation. This isn't meant to be for the sake of being awkward (well, maybe it is), but explore, probe, understand and eventually expand upon what is in the brief.'

Just make sure you question the brief in an intelligent, professional way. Use the five handy words that make up the SMART acronym as a checklist. Ask yourself: Is the deadline too short? Perhaps you need to ask your creative director to press for an extension to the deadline. Is the product itself ready to be launched? What about the budget? Is the objective attainable within the set budget? The size of the budget is a key factor in setting the objective.

THE BUDGET DETERMINES THE OBJECTIVE

In the American Airlines example, we saw that because it's such a big client, the objective could be ambitious, as there was sufficient money to reach the target audience in this highly competitive market, in a variety of mainstream media. A generous budget gives the planner, as well as you, the creative team, the opportunity to think big, and to carry the objective through in the most effective ways. However, don't be dazzled by a big budget and go off in several different directions: the key thing is to stay focused on the objective. Every medium should be used to its best advantage to serve the objective.

The scope of the campaign depends on what the client wants to spend. Since American Airlines is a major airline, the planner in this example could set an ambitious objective which could be realized in a national campaign. In fact, American Airlines ran a large, fully integrated campaign from magazines to mobiles, explaining the options in a special advertising feature, offering in-flight and post-flight benefits via smartphone devices on mobiles – all answering the same objective: to enable travellers to control their time.

Mobiles, for example, deliver up-to-the-minute flight information, as well as your boarding pass, so there's no need to print it out.

When you're working in a freelance capacity, the client might not initially reveal their budget, thinking that once you know the budget, you will spend more than you otherwise would. However, you need a rough idea of what your client can (or wants to) spend before you can set a realistic objective to determine the role for your advertising. Be brave. Insist on a budget before you commit to a freelance project. That way you won't waste your time.

LOOK AT THE BIGGER PICTURE

Just as you considered various key aspects of your own life to set each personal objective, the client and agency look beyond advertising issues before setting the objective. You'll recall in Chapter One a discussion of wider issues identified by the acronym 'PESTEL': political, economic, societal, technological, environmental and legal. Everyone in advertising needs to keep aware of what's going on in the world so that the 'conversation' with the consumer reflects an understanding of their situation.

AN ADVERTISING OBJECTIVE IS ALWAYS 'CONSUMER-FACING'

The advertising objective speaks to the consumer far more directly than a marketing objective. No one, for example, would expect consumer advertising to solve a pricing, or distribution problem.

HOW ADVERTISING AND MARKETING ROLES DIFFER

Marketing issues are important. They include aspects of the product or service itself, distribution, pricing, promotional activity and the competition. A marketing objective relates to, but is not the same as, the advertising objective. For example, suppose that Amazon wants to increase its sales of the Kindle. Its marketing department, together with the agency, decide that supermarkets would provide an excellent opportunity.

A valid marketing objective would be: 'to increase sales of the Kindle at Christmas in selected supermarkets'.

Related to this marketing aim would be an advertising objective that would speak directly to the consumer.

For example:

To make the Kindle an integral part of your Christmas cooking. The advertising objective would be aimed at the supermarket shopper who is buying ingredients for festive recipes. The Kindle would be the perfect gift for the cook of the house.

The strategy, the 'how' of it, might be to pre-load festive recipes onto the Kindle specifically for this Christmas push. Success, in terms of sales, would depend on many things going according to plan: the advertising campaign, and also the marketing activity, including distribution, any promotional activity such as in-store demonstrations, all the online information, as well as relationship marketing with relevant brands of food and drink.

For a brand to succeed, there needs to be an overarching, common goal. If you work on national or global advertising, your creative solutions will form part of this wider relationship. As consumers, we sense whether this relationship is seamless, or a jumble of unconnected parts. Imagine, for example, that you see a witty, clever TV commercial one evening. The next day you click on the brand's website and find that it has a different campaign line, with no related imagery or the witty tone of voice which you responded to the previous evening. That would spell trouble for the brand. Why not start a list of brands that you think are getting it right?

Let your feet fly.

AVE

The debate continues about the environmental impact of different modes of transportation. The objective of this motivating Spanish ad is to convince its audience to 'fly' via high-speed trains.

Marketing and advertising strategies could be combined to boost sales of the Kindle at Christmas by pre-loading the Kindle with festive recipes and then advertising it to supermarket shoppers as the first ingredient for a delicious feast.

ALL OBJECTIVES REQUIRE CLARITY

One of the most difficult things for a planner, or for you, if you're working freelance, is to take a lot of information and synthesize it into a clear, single-minded objective. However, some objectives are easier to write than others. For example, the Fiat commercial by Leo Burnett, 'Chess Game' (opposite), has a simple objective: 'to offer customers zero per cent interest financing for a limited time only'. The resulting creative work is witty and clever, using the game of chess as a metaphor. The advice offered to the viewer is to seize the moment and take up the zero per cent finance deal. Note how it's the older player who seizes the moment.

LAUNCHING A COMPLEX NEW PRODUCT REQUIRES THE CLEAREST OBJECTIVE OF ALL

It's difficult to arrive at a clear, single-minded objective for a complex product entering a challenging market. Yet, it's extremely important to achieve that clarity of purpose if the launch is to succeed.

Often, the immediate impulse on the part of a client when asking the agency to advertise a complex product is to try to achieve several objectives at once, and to explain everything in every ad. That inevitably results in unclear communication and risks confusing the consumer.

Each of the two product launches we will look at in the following pages – the Apple Macintosh personal computer and *The Independent* newspaper – sets an ambitious objective within a complex category.

Viewers, as well as ad-industry professionals, regard Apple's '1984', by the American agency Chiat/Day, as one of the most memorable and successful TV commercials of all time. Inspired by George Orwell's novel of the same name, how did '1984', shown only twice, make such an impact worldwide, and come to symbolize Apple's overall objective for decades to come? (You can view this commercial online by typing into your search engine: 'Apple 1984'.)

What was the objective? Was it, simply, to launch a new computer? It was more complex than that, yet the objective still had to be distilled into a clear aim.

According to Lee Clow, as reported in a 2004 article in *Macworld* by Adelia Cellini, the original objective was 'to show the fight for the control of computer technology as a struggle of the few against the many'.

A STRUGGLE OF THE FEW AGAINST THE MANY

This objective reflects an understanding of the computer market at the time, as well as an insight into the potential consumer for this new personal computer. The

objective set the controversial, risky tone for this striking launch. Its attitude resonated instantly with the 'few' design-oriented, creative people who would, in fact, grow in number to become millions of loyal consumers over the years.

WHO WERE THE MANY?

It's easy to forget who the 'Big Brother' was, against whom Apple pitted their objective. Was it Microsoft? When Steve Jobs, in his 1983 Apple keynote address, showed a preview of the commercial to a select audience, he commented: 'It is now 1984. It appears IBM wants it all. Apple is perceived to be the only hope to offer IBM a run for its money.'

Shot by film director Ridley Scott, this Apple commercial, '1984', was created by Steve Hayden (copywriter), Brent Thomas (art director) and Lee Clow (creative director) at the American agency Chiat/Day.

1   3

2

IBM was the arch rival at the time, and Apple's objective clearly set out to vanquish their hold on the market. This one commercial, whose approach became synonymous with Apple's image, was named by *Advertising Age* as the 1980s *Commercial of the Decade.*

As it turned out, the George Orwell estate and the television company which held the rights to Orwell's novel considered the commercial an infringement of copyright, so the commercial was shown on TV only twice. In spite of its meagre official airtime, the commercial was re-broadcasted by news programmes as soon as it launched. And thanks to the internet, it has since been viewed millions of times – an early example of viral advertising.

THE OBJECTIVE STEERS WHAT FOLLOWS

A well-defined objective is like the true north of a compass. It sets the direction for everything which follows. The resulting creative work will then be single-minded and powerful. This was especially true of the launch, in 1986, of the British newspaper *The Independent*. According to Clare Rossi, then Saatchi planner, now at Ogilvy, the launch objective was for people 'to make a statement' about themselves when they chose to read *The Independent*. She continues: 'We were throwing down the gauntlet, and asking people to prove they were independent.'

The initial poster did exactly that. Art-directed by Digby Atkinson, who wanted to make the whole campaign 'as challenging as possible', the poster featured an image of the rolled-up newspaper, facing potential readers with the simple rhetorical question, written by Peter Russell: 'It is. Are you?'

Which came first, the objective – to make a statement about being independent – or the name? Tim Mellors, then Saatchi creative group head, and now Grey's worldwide creative director, says, rather surprisingly, that it was one of 200 potential names, including *The Globe*, *The Nation* and *The Meridian*. But *The Independent* 'researched really well … now that it's the name of the paper, everyone says it could not have been anything else.'

1   The memorable question that launched the campaign for *The Independent* newspaper wouldn't have worked with any other name. 'But it was one of a whole raft of ideas', according to Tim Mellors. The choice of name then became synonymous with the idea, or concept, of the newspaper itself.

2   The advertising objective was met not by running magazine ads with long copy, or features highlighting journalists writing for the new paper, but by inviting like-minded people to join the new community of readers.

3   The paper's independent stance still appears on its banner: 'FREE FROM PARTY POLITICAL TIES | FREE FROM PROPRIETORIAL INFLUENCE'.

1
2   3

UPDATING THE OBJECTIVE FOR 'i'

As readers migrated to online and digested versions of their newspapers, a new, shorter version of *The Independent*, called *i*, was launched in 2010. It had the following objective: 'to convince the public that *i* marks a new concept in newspapers – an intelligent, fast read for time-poor commuters'.

Created by Trevor Beattie of London agency Beattie McGuinness Bungay (BMB), the poster campaign ran a series of copy lines answering that objective, among them: '*i* is all you need in the time you have'; '*i* is all you need for 20p'; '*i* is 20p'; and a grammatically challenging reinvention of the original question: '*i* is are you?'

1   The objective clearly set out what the advertising campaign had to achieve. And it did so, with a witty, intelligent, award-winning campaign, using TV and outdoor.

2   The complexity of the product, in that it's full of different views every day, meant that a pared-down approach aimed at the potential reader's attitude, was the best way forward.

3   *The Independent* attracted a circulation of over 400,000 copies by 1989, without showing anything more than a rolled-up newspaper. The Sunday edition was subsequently launched in 1990.

4   The advertising for *i*, a digested version of *The Independent*, picked up the language from the original campaign, maintaining the overall brand personality.

4

DEFINING THE OBJECTIVE FOR THE FIGURE 8 YOGHURT BRIEF

Consider what you've learned about writing the objective and return to the yoghurt creative brief. The client has discussed with the agency that they would like more men to enjoy low-fat Figure 8 yoghurt. At the moment, research groups reveal that men are trying Shape, the low-fat Figure 8 product aimed at women, and liking it more than the other low-fat ranges. However, they are not buying it for themselves. It isn't a distribution problem. It's an image problem. Figure 8 is aimed specifically at women.

Often, you start with a line of thinking, take it through the brief, and then go back to see which elements need refining, or changing. So we could start with the objective below, continue to write the rest of the creative brief, and see if the strategy we come up with justifies staying with this ambitious objective.

To encourage men to buy low-fat Figure 8 yoghurt for themselves.
Advertising objectives often address issues of image. In this case, it's not the image of the brand that needs changing; it's the self-image of the men who eat it but don't buy it. Another way to phrase the objective might be:

To make it acceptable for a man to buy Figure 8 in spite of its feminine image.
But is this still too ambitious? Is there another way to write it? Think back to the American Airlines advertising.

Could the objective offer a bit more insight into the male audience, in order to lead more quickly to a more distinctive strategy? A good creative brief should help you work quickly and well. For example:

To encourage a man not to resist buying low-fat Figure 8 for himself.
This objective shows greater understanding of the research. We know that men like Figure 8 more than the low-fat brands aimed at them. This objective makes it clearer what the advertising must achieve. Note that it's easier to think about your target audience if you talk to one person at a time. This takes us to our next chapter.

3. TARGET MARKET

WHO IS THE PRIMARY FOCUS OF YOUR ADVERTISING?

The purpose of this section of the creative brief is to enable you to identify and understand the people to whom you need to direct your advertising. To determine the scope and nature of the target market, planners access various forms of research, then analyse and interpret the findings to give you relevant information and insight into the individuals who make up this primary group. Who exactly are they? What age? Which competitors' products are they buying now? These are basic questions.

A further set of questions, more difficult to answer, and arguably more important, relates to the nature of the individuals within the group. What are these people really like? What is their attitude to aspects of their lives which could influence their response to your advertising? Here, your own research into character can add insight to what the planner provides. Only by understanding how people think and feel can you form a strategy, and create ads that respond to their needs and desires.

The group might be quite diverse, yet a common need or desire that transcends these differences is what draws each of them to your client's product or service. For example, the Samsonite luggage ad, 'Heaven and Hell' (above), created by JWT Shanghai, shows passengers enjoying a 'heavenly' flight in an airy, cloud-filled cabin, while their luggage is piled in the hold below, depicted in red to represent hell. This imaginative visual dramatizes how Samsonite, a brand of luggage known for decades for its virtually indestructible qualities, survives the lurid 'hell' of air travel unscathed.

The ad is aimed at well-heeled Chinese air travellers. Although they may differ in terms of age, gender, occupation, even income (although their income level will be well above China's average citizen), they all value their possessions and share a desire for smart-looking luggage designed to protect those possessions. Once you identify this shared attitude as a defining characteristic of these travellers, you are in a much better position to create effective, creative advertising.

This ad for Samsonite vividly contrasts travellers' 'heavenly' time above with their suitcases' 'hellish' trip down below, emphasizing the ability of Samsonite suitcases to withstand tough conditions. In 2011, 'Heaven and Hell' became the first Chinese ad ever to win the Grand Prix at the Cannes Lions Festival.

IDENTIFYING THE PRIMARY TARGET MARKET

Detective work is how strategic thinker Chris Forrest, founder of The Nursery Research and Planning (www.the-nursery.net) and former planning director at London's Duckworth Finn Grubb Waters, describes the planner's role. They're always asking questions and searching for answers, essentially within three consumer-focused areas: what is the consumer's relationship with the category, with the brand itself, and with existing advertising?

The planner begins the process of identifying the target market by investigating what the client already knows about the market, and the people who currently buy their product. The amount of available information depends on the size and sophistication of the client's marketing department. Planners will seek answers from quantitative, data-based research, as well as from qualitative research, which includes consumer interviews and focus sessions. Larger clients depend on ongoing tracking studies to measure buying habits, and to assess brand strength and advertising effectiveness. Smaller clients use these tools more sporadically, so the information is not as robust.

FOCUS ON THE INDIVIDUAL

Your primary audience is made up of individuals, who, if described in demographic terms, are identified according to age, gender, income and occupation. ('Demographic' comes from the Greek words *demos*, meaning 'people', and *graphos*, meaning 'something drawn', so demographics can be seen as a picture of a group of people.) A planner's role is to liaise with the client to supply you with these statistics. They can tell you a lot. But they only go so far. You will see later in the chapter how a segmentation study can be invaluable.

If you always treat your audience as just a set of statistics, they become like a bunch of stick figures without minds and hearts. This approach makes it hard for you to see that every group is composed of living, breathing individuals. You need to understand how to communicate a shared desire to a diverse group. How to interest them in considering a different approach to an important issue. Effective advertising must strike a chord with one person at a time to achieve any kind of positive response.

REACH OUT TO THE CONSUMER. ENGAGE!

The dilemma, or challenge, depending on how you look at it, is no longer how to reach an individual, but with what content. Social media, such as Facebook and Twitter, as well as any web-based advertising, plus mobile and email marketing, including the ever-expanding world of apps, offer you a tantalizing variety of opportunities to reach people on an individual basis. So it's easy to think that 'reaching out' to someone equals 'engaging' with them. You need a real connection

Meet your very own personal trainer

Personal trainers don't have to be bossy. All your baby asks is that you keep him fed and clean. In exchange your baby helps you burn 500 calories each day.

Breastfeeding is the best way to lose those post-pregnancy pounds, and a great way to keep you and your baby happy and healthy.

To learn more about the benefits of breastfeeding visit bestbeginnings.info.

best
beginnings
Nurture yourself skin

to engage with someone, shared interests, an offering of something. Naturally, most clients want to reach out to consumers and engage with them. They always have done.

However, many clients, and their agencies, make this mistake of confusing 'reaching out' to the consumer and 'engaging' with them. Of course, anyone who has received scores of 'junk' – i.e. insufficiently targeted – emails will know that they are not the same thing. In fact, email marketing is increasingly thought by people in the industry to be less effective than other forms of digital advertising because it is too intrusive and fails to capture an individual's attention with an attractive offering (as opposed to a useful app, or a branded game that you enjoy playing).

What about the images that appear on your Facebook page with links to what you, in particular, do or 'like'? Even if yours is a niche activity or interest, increasingly sophisticated software is constantly picking up on details in your own posts and those of your friends with shared interests. Maybe they're not all things that hit the mark, but the picture you build of your life on social media enables the software to come close enough with suggestions you're likely to engage with.

ENGAGING A PERSON VIA SOCIAL MEDIA

Sophisticated analysis programs enable advertisers to reach *into* the daily, dynamic world of social media, then reach *out to* a particular person, having identified products and services that have a very good chance of engaging with particular aspects of that person's life. Let's suppose you practise yoga, or indeed teach it. Our example, Josie, is an actor, as well as a professional yoga teacher. The links that appear on Josie's Facebook page take her to products, places and events connected to her daily life.

Some links are far more obvious than others. Yoga t-shirts, for example. Whereas

The primary focus for this Design & Art Direction (D&AD) competition brief is young potential parents. The objective is to convey that breastfeeding (as opposed to formula milk) is a positive choice for them to make when they are bringing up their baby.

Anouk Robert Tissot and Joe Talboys created this winning solution. Health professionals around the UK have been distributing this highly targeted postcard to new mothers since 2011.

the UK Japanese Embassy Facebook page, also linked from Josie's Facebook page, is a bit of a lateral jump from yoga, with its Indian, Hindu roots. It is nonetheless a clever one. Josie is a world traveller, and that information on her Facebook page, combined with her professional yoga practice, might be what led the software to make the connection between tranquillity and meditation and Japan. Perhaps cultural events sponsored by the Japanese Embassy would interest Josie. She might like to visit Japan on her next trip. Although she's been to India, she's never been to Japan, and might not have seriously considered it until the link appeared on her page.

Facebook's 'Timeline' feature is a new way of aggregating the images you like and want to share. This offers another opportunity for companies to reach out and engage with consumers who 'like' their products. Simply capture an image from the company and put it on your Facebook page. It's branded, so your friends and relatives will see it.

MAKE THE MESSAGE PERSONAL

Whether or not clients are successful in engaging our interest in a particular product or service depends not on which medium is used to reach us, but on how well the client and their advertising agency understand what we like, want or need. As a creative, you need to explore the potential of each medium and use it to its best advantage, whether it's an ad, app, email or branded content. Crucially, the client has to follow through on whatever promises are made in the advertising.

Lakeland is an established high-street kitchenware company which uses digital media effectively. They offer tempting photos of what you can make with their baking utensils for you to brighten up your Facebook 'Timeline'. The photos carry the company logo.

Banks and investment companies are notorious for not catering to their customers on a personal level unless they happen to have an extremely high net worth. Agency EuroRSCG New York created a successful campaign for Charles Schwab (see overleaf), an American investment company, based on the understanding that a person who is investing money, whether a little or a lot, wants personal service. It sounds obvious. Yet most investment companies, like banks, cater on a truly personal level only to larger investors.

The advertising copy – 'Some places give you a welcome packet. We give you a welcome person.' – reassures potential customers that they will be dealt with personally. Their overtly friendly 'talk to Chuck' logo reinforces this personal approach. It's risky for a serious firm to sound so casual. A risk worth taking. The company presents a human face, promising that 'your own dedicated person' will talk to you one to one. This simple approach makes an even greater impact in today's digital world where so much banking, insurance and other financial transactions are conducted over the phone or on the internet, without any direct human interaction. Print is a good medium for this straightforward approach, reinforcing the timeless, priceless and old-fashioned value of two people discussing something important, face to face.

LEARN FROM CONSUMER-GENERATED ADVERTISING

It's always worthwhile looking at consumer-generated ads because the way they involve their current target audience can teach you a lot. The theory of this type of advertising is that the direct involvement of the target audience makes the communication 'real'. More believable. A good example is a US ad for the Citi credit card, which features an image of a dog asleep with a cuddly toy (see overleaf).

The advertising copy is based on a Citibank customer's experience and tells the story of how the owner and her husband believed their dog was lonely and tried a lot of different ways to cheer him up, finally solving the problem by buying him a cuddly toy. The story appeals to dog owners whether they're Citibank customers or not. It's an altogether successful approach and a far cry from the staid advertising which banks used to run decades ago.

HOW DOES SOMEONE ELSE THINK AND FEEL?

When you're sitting at your desk in an agency, you and your creative partner can feel distanced from the personal world of the individual whom you're trying to talk to. Especially if his or her life is different from yours. The planner, and you, need to explore how a person thinks and feels about aspects of their life. Demographic information is just the beginning of what is needed to gain an insight into an individual who forms part of your primary target market. You always need to go deeper.

1   2

USE YOUR IMAGINATION

Imagination is central to generating ideas and creating advertising. However, prior to that, you need to use your gift to imagine another person's life. To walk in his or her shoes. How you imagine someone else's life can't be the stuff of pure fantasy. It must stem from the facts you and your planner have gathered. From talking and listening to people in your target audience. From interpretation. We're in the midst of the most consumer-focused advertising there has ever been, yet understanding someone else isn't easy. Social media seems to reveal everything people are thinking and doing, from one minute to the next. But it's still hard to get inside someone else's head.

THINK OF YOURSELF AS A DETECTIVE

Whether or not you're working with a planner, it helps to think of yourself as a detective as well. To gain an understanding of your primary target audience, keep in mind the consumer-focused aspects mentioned earlier: what is the person's relationship with the category, with the brand itself, and with existing advertising?

Begin your detective work from the point of view of the individual who is within your primary target market. For example, is the person experiencing a new challenge that your product or service can help with?

To find out how that individual feels, you would ideally want to talk first hand to someone in that position. That's what a planner would do. One-to-one interviews conducted by your planner won't be something you can share, but you can conduct your own informal interviews. Think about the people you know. A friend of your parents? A relative? Someone in your neighbourhood who could

1   Euro RSCG New York created this successful campaign, which urges investors to switch from their current brokerage and to 'talk to Chuck'. Its simplicity is persuasive and refreshing.

2   This consumer-generated ad for the Citi card is warm, and raises a smile. It invites readers to tell their story, drawing them into Citibank's friendly circle.

3&4   The primary focus in these examples for business-software company Intuit are the people who run small businesses. Everything about this ad reassures the overworked small-business person. The shop in the ad is able to present itself as calm and organized – thanks to Intuit. This shows an understanding of the target market – running a small business may be frantic, but should never look that way to the customer.

3

4

spare half an hour of their time? Draw up a list of questions. If you're working as a team, one of you can take notes. Ask if you can record the conversation. Listen to how their day is spent. Even a short interview with a person or people who represent your target market can make a brief come to life.

LEARN WHAT MAGAZINES KNOW ABOUT THEIR READERS

Magazines spend a great deal of time and money learning everything they can about their readers. If you're going to communicate with someone, you need to understand what he or she is interested in. Find out which are their favourite magazines. Read them carefully – the ads and the articles. Each magazine provides you with an insight into a person who might be quite different from you in age and interests – and gender. Also, access the magazine's media kit. It's free. You can learn valuable information on the demographic and behavioural nature of the magazine's primary target. Media kits are online or available from a magazine's advertising department.

If your target market reads this magazine, so should you. What do its readers like? What don't they like? Why?

KEEP YOUR EYES AND EARS OPEN

Some people walk down the street and notice everything. Others notice very little. Frank Lowe, legendary advertising figure who worked in the UK and US and founded Lowe & Partners, gave this valuable advice to account people, the essence of which has just as much relevance to creatives.

'All too often, I have found that people in our business, having reached a position of some importance, remove themselves to a large property in the country as far away as possible from the consumers they are talking to. This is self-evidently foolish. How can you talk to people if you don't know how they live?' (*Dear Lord Leverhulme, I Think We May Have Solved Your Problem*, by Frank Lowe).

The award-winning 'Beautify Your City' campaign (see opposite) by Colenso BBDO New Zealand targeted businesses in the central business district of Auckland. It came about from the agency people looking hard at their city and thinking of ways to reduce the amount of rubbish piled up in the business district and to make that which remained look an awful lot better. Planner James Hurman explains how the 360° campaign worked, from curbing illegal dumping by placing flowerbeds on targeted areas, to educating businesses with a kit delivered by council ambassadors. Each business owner in the business district received bin bags printed with an attractive leafy design. Auckland's streets were transformed overnight.

Rubbish is never going to disappear, but advertising agency Colenso BBDO found a way to make it beautiful. They turned the ordinary rubbish bag into a bushy hedge, which formed garden beds when placed curbside. The 'Beautify Your City' campaign was created to make Auckland a more beautiful city. It prevented illegal dumping by placing flowerbeds on targeted areas and educated businesses, with a kit delivered by council ambassadors.

ONLINE SOURCES

If you're working in an agency without planners, or freelance, you won't have a research budget to fund you. Although you cannot replicate all the quantitative, data-based research undertaken by large agencies and their clients, there is a great deal of research that you can carry out online. The web is bursting with information. Enter a well-defined subject into your search engine and follow the rich trail of information, from Wikipedia, to government sites, opinion polls and consumer surveys on product performance, many of which, depending on the country, are in the public domain.

SOCIAL MEDIA

Social media is a great source of individual opinion on just about everything. Choose carefully. Don't put too much emphasis on one view. Follow blogs of people you admire, both in and out of the advertising industry, and whose views reveal insight. Log on to community sites. Join the conversation. Ask pertinent questions, and evaluate the replies. You could begin your own blog and create a lively following.

TARGET GROUP INDEX

Accessing specialist statistical surveys involves substantial subscription fees. However, sections of some of these sources are free. Foremost among the sources of consumer-oriented data is Target Group Index: TGI (http://globaltgi.com). This powerful marketing tool began in the UK in 1969 and now covers 60 countries. Its top-line information is free.

TGI carries out consumer surveys and provides an ongoing source of knowledge on consumers' buying habits, as well as on their interests, attitudes to various aspects of their lives, their motivations, and what media they consume.

Planners have used TGI for years for its statistical, quantitative data and behavioural, qualitative information. TGI goes one step further by providing cross-referencing of the information. It's this cross-tabulation which makes the difference, enabling you to identify several different clusters of people within a particular target market who have similar attitudes and behaviour.

This is called a segmentation study – you can look at a segment of a particular market and see how a certain group's attitude and behaviour corresponds to its brand preferences, buying habits, media consumption, etc. A segmentation study typically divides a target market into four or more sub-groups defined by behaviour and/or attitude, such as Restrained, Materialistic, Aesthetic and Adventurous, rather than categorizing people according to demographic characteristics – their age, income, education and status or job.

The theory behind this method of research and analysis is the belief that people who share attitudes and behaviour have more in common with each other (and thus form logical clusters) than people who are the same age, or earn the same income.

Market segmentation enables a company and its advertising agency to achieve a much better understanding of two things: what consumers within each cluster would respond to in terms of a product or service; and how to communicate effectively with that cluster.

To arrive at this information, the research would be in-depth (focus groups or individual interviews), to learn about a person's attitudes and beliefs, as well as wide-ranging: quantitative studies to test the various approaches, whether it's a new product introduction, or a new advertising campaign.

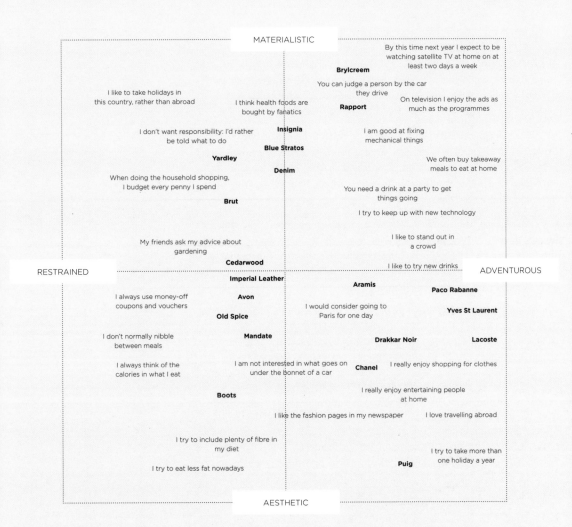

MATERIALISTIC

By this time next year I expect to be
watching satellite TV at home on at
least two days a week

Brylcreem

You can judge a person by the car
they drive

I like to take holidays in
this country, rather than abroad

I think health foods are
bought by fanatics

Rapport

On television I enjoy the ads as
much as the programmes

I don't want responsibility: I'd rather
be told what to do

Insignia

I am good at fixing
mechanical things

Blue Stratos

Yardley

Denim

We often buy takeaway
meals to eat at home

When doing the household shopping,
I budget every penny I spend

You need a drink at a party to get
things going

Brut

I try to keep up with new technology

My friends ask my advice about
gardening

I like to stand out in
a crowd

Cedarwood

I like to try new drinks

RESTRAINED

Imperial Leather

ADVENTUROUS

Aramis

Paco Rabanne

I always use money-off
coupons and vouchers

Avon

I would consider going to
Paris for one day

Yves St Laurent

Old Spice

I don't normally nibble
between meals

Mandate

Drakkar Noir

Lacoste

I always think of the
calories in what I eat

I am not interested in what goes on
under the bonnet of a car

Chanel

I really enjoy shopping for clothes

I really enjoy entertaining people
at home

Boots

I like the fashion pages in my newspaper

I love travelling abroad

I try to include plenty of fibre in
my diet

I try to take more than
one holiday a year

Puig

I try to eat less fat nowadays

AESTHETIC

The 'Global TGI Barometer' is another helpful feature of the TGI site. It gives you a snapshot of topical articles, and of how these issues are affecting consumers. The TGI Barometer indicates how the wind is blowing, enabling you to empathize with how your audience is feeling at the moment. Only when you're aware of the external factors people are reacting to, or coping with, can you hope to engage their interest. Subjects include: 'For recession marketing, think thrifty', 'Are traditional family values dying out?', 'Flying: the environmental debate', 'Working nine to five', 'Calorie-counting consumers: dieting around the globe', 'The global wine market', 'Giving credit to consumers', 'Charitable donations', 'The charms of chocolate'. The list is rich and varied. You can use any information from TGI, as long as you credit the source: Target Group Index © Kantar Media 2011.

INTERPRET THE RESEARCH

The skill of a planner is in asking the right questions and interpreting the research. You will see as you do your own research that there is rarely a shortage of data. It's the interpretation of the data, the analysis of them, that leads to an insight.

For example, most clients know who their main competitor is. Yet, relying only on this knowledge can lead to unwise decisions: either to look for a different target market, or to suggest a strategy that tries to persuade your competitor's target market to switch brands. A skilled planner will analyse the data on consumers' buying habits and then go deeper, into qualitative research, perhaps one-to-one interviews. This yields clues.

For example, in many product categories, a person possesses a 'portfolio' of brands, meaning that a person responds positively to more than one brand's approach within a category. It isn't this OR that. It's this AND that. Your own experience probably reveals this: how many different brands of trainers do you own? Chances are, you buy more than one brand.

Consider the well-heeled Chinese air traveller – the primary target focus for the Samsonite ad 'Heaven and Hell'. What if research revealed that he or she already owns another expensive brand of luggage, perhaps Bric's, and is very happy with it. This elegant, Italian-based global brand advertises in a very different way from Samsonite.

Their most recent 'Love is ...' campaign doesn't mention the features of their luggage. Their strategy is not to highlight sturdiness, even though the exquisitely made Bric's brand of luggage stands up to some rough treatment. Instead, it projects a romantic image of the glorious world of travel, exemplified in the ad opposite for their Signature Collection with its campaign line *'Viaggiate, con fantasia'* ('Travel, with imagination'). The owner of Bric's luggage might also be attracted to Samsonite – a very different type of luggage, yet still desirable in its own way.

Perhaps a traveller would choose the Bric's Signature Collection carry-on trolley case for one trip, Samsonite for another. Or a traveller might use a combination of both luggage brands on the same trip. He or she doesn't want or need to 'switch' brands. So the primary target group could arguably continue to buy Bric's, a brand they are very pleased with, as well as buying, maybe for the first time, Samsonite, thus responding positively to both campaigns. By focusing on the same primary target market as the competitor, but using a different strategy according to the brand's strengths, the agency would be making the right decision.

People own a 'portfolio' of brands in many categories – for example, luggage, watches, clothes, shoes and cosmetics. A competitor's target market might also be the primary focus of your advertising. The strategy can differ according to the brand. Bric's focuses on the elegance of its luggage, whereas Samsonite stresses durability. The same traveller might well respond to both of these strategies and own luggage from both brands. Here, Bric's is set against a view of the Villa del Balbianello, on Lake Como, Italy.

Lago di Como - Villa del Balbianello - Si ringrazia il FAI

www.brics.lt

100%
made in italy
material

VIAGGIATE, CON FANTASIA.

A group so diverse and dynamic
as 16–24 year-old Brits
deserves a modern approach
to market segmentation.

Meet the Tribes

We stay close to them through a broad ethnographic focus
on their unifying and divisive activities and attitudes.

We then draw together a deeply insightful snapshot which
allows us to segment youth accurately, and brands
to reach them successfully. This time we identified
23 tribes interacting as part of five larger groups.

Mainstream

_Townies

_Chavs

_Sports Junkies

_Casuals

_Boy Racers

_Ravers

_Streets Rats

Alternative

_Skaters

_Metalheads

_Emos

_Young Alts

_Scene Kids

_Gamers

Urban

_Get Paid Crew

_Blingers

_Trackies

_DIYers

Aspirant
Mainstream

_Trendies

_Rahs

Leading

_Geek

_Ind

_Hi

_C

UK TRIBES

The youth market is a difficult one to understand and talk to, even if you're part of it. As a way of gaining knowledge and insight about their potential viewers, the Audience, Technologies & Insight team at Channel 4, have worked for five years to put together a highly informative, and entertaining website called UK Tribes: (www.uktribes.com). Neil Taylor, senior research executive, invites you to search the full content of the site using the password: iblametheparents. It's all free.

The campaign line, 'The home of UK youth research', tells you what you'll find: a comprehensive description and analysis of the UK youth landscape, segmented into 23 'tribes', as described by young people themselves. The site focuses on youth in the UK. However, it offers a valuable window on young people across Europe, and further afield, because of the ethnically diverse student population in the UK, and the lively interchange of youth culture via the worlds of music, gaming and social media.

FLUIDITY AMONG GROUPS

The 23 tribes detailed in the image shown, interact as part of five larger groups: Mainstream, Alternative, Urban, Aspirant Mainstream and Leading Edge. Andy Crysell of Crowd DNA, the company that conducted the research, emphasizes the fluidity and exchange of ideas among these 23 tribes. They are not fixed, any more than the four quadrants we looked at earlier in the TGI analysis describe mutually exclusive characteristics. Whenever you look at segmentation studies, whether of younger or older people, you have to cross-reference the attitude with your client's product or service. For example, someone might be Mainstream (or traditional) when it comes to clothes, yet Leading Edge (or adventurous) with cars.

Researchers asked two key questions: what unifies these 23 tribes and what divides them? View and hear answers from 80 young people and learn more about how they think and feel on the site's video-blogging element: uktribes.com/videoblogs.

It features 16–24 year olds from the various groups talking about five topics: Hopes and Fears, Identity, Brands, Gaming, and Leisure. These are all important areas for anyone in the communications business to think about, especially when addressing this young target market.

A WORKING TEMPLATE: WHO ARE YOU?

This template, which you'll find at the back of the book, gives you a framework to help pull together and distil what you've learned about your primary target market. Remember to retain your focus on the person most likely to be attracted to your message. That person represents your target market. There will always be people outside this primary circle who see your advertising. However, if they're only mildly interested in the particular category of your client's product or service, their response will be too sporadic to focus on.

Whether you are writing your own brief or you are given the brief, perhaps on work placement, expanding the description of the target market into the three sections of the 'Who Are You?' template helps you to understand the person to whom you're talking.

Each of the three sections has guiding questions.

In summary, the first section encourages you to create a character sketch, to give a name to the person who most closely represents your target market. The second section asks you to speak conversationally with that person, offering the promise or benefit which you think will interest this individual. The third step involves thinking about the 'where' of the advertising – the media. To make it more likely that he or she will respond positively, it helps to consider what mood the person is going to be in wherever they 'bump' into your message.

These sections illustrate the interlocking nature of the whole creative brief process, how the understanding of your target audience influences the strategy, the tone of voice and the choice of media – all subsequent sections of the creative brief.

CREATIVE BRIEF TEMPLATE

PRODUCT/ SERVICE

Amstel Pulse.

OBJECTIVE

To get people to try the new filtered beer from Amstel - Amstel Pulse.

TARGET MARKET

18–35 year-old men.

Specifically - Matt Thompson. 27. Manchester.

SUPPORT

1. Filtered – means removing the bad flavours.

2. Modern, clear glass bottle – so you can see what you are drinking.

3. Ring-pull bottle opening – means you can drink it anywhere.

STRATEGY

By showing Matt that Amstel pulse is filtered to remove bad taste.

PROPOSITION

Amstel Pulse. Micro filtered to ensure good taste.

COMPETITION

Grolsch, Tuborg, Peroni Nastro Azzuro, Left, Corona, Sol, Budweiser, Coors, Pilsner Urquell, Desperados, other beers, ciders and wines.

MANDATORY ELEMENTS

Packshot.

TONE OF VOICE

Non-traditional, modern, simple.

DESIRED CONSUMER RESPONSE

Hah, removing bad taste. Anything that does that has got to be good – I'll give it a try.

MEDIA REQUIREMENT

Print, press, digital.

CASE STUDY:
AMSTEL PULSE

Creative team Ed Ryder and Bryan Stewart devised their own brief for Amstel Pulse as part of their final portfolio on the MA Creative Advertising course at University College Falmouth. They wrote the 'Who Are You?' for their primary target audience, and from it created the advertising campaign which follows on. It's witty and fresh, and speaks directly to their primary target audience. The team is now at the advertising agency 180 Amsterdam.

WHO ARE YOU?

PRODUCT: AMSTEL PULSE

Describe the person you're talking to. It could be someone you know, or you could create an imaginary character. It has to be someone interested in your proposition. Give this person a good name, so that you have a clear picture in your mind.
Matt Thompson. 27. Manchester. Geography teacher in a secondary school. He is interested in design, lifestyle magazines, fashion and modern trends. He reads about them whenever he can. He is dedicated to his profession and usually does a couple of hours' work when he comes home. He then relaxes at home, watches some TV or reads.

Decide what you want to say. What promise or benefit can you offer that you believe will genuinely interest the person you've described. Don't try to be clever at this point. You're not writing copy, just deciding what is your best offer. If you don't have a unique selling point, you could have an emotional selling point. Write as clearly and briefly as you can, in a conversational tone. Think of it as an email to a friend, or colleague.
Amstel Pulse is a beer that is filtered so it removes the elements associated with bad taste, leaving only good taste.

Imagine precisely how and where the promise or benefit you're making will connect with the person you're talking to. Where will s/he 'bump' into your message as the day unfolds. What mood will this person be in when your message reaches them? Are they too busy to pay attention? Perhaps you need to rethink some aspect of your medium. Why not draw a graph of their day. Now you'll begin to see how the product or service you have to offer fits into that individual's life. Once you understand this, you're ready to talk to this person, in the appropriate medium and with an involving approach.

Matt gets up in the morning, quite late. Gets ready as quickly as possible. He drives from his apartment and gets to the school early enough. At

Hilton
Paris
Paris Hilton

Sandals
Socks
Socks + Sandals

Amstel Pulse. Micro filtered to ensure good taste

Amstel Pulse. Micro filtered to ensure good taste

break and lunchtime he usually catches up on some more work.

After a stressful, but enjoyable day he drives home and he may see some of our outdoor executions. In the evening he watches TV on demand. He spends some time online if he can, planning his holiday trips, looking for the best deals.

He is quite prepared. He wants to get the most out of his holiday time. He may see our online execution here, which he will actively engage with out of curiosity. At the weekend when he is out shopping he will see our six sheet executions, which he will hopefully identify with. This will make him laugh, and later that night he will see them again when he goes out with his friends.

He may even try an Amstel Pulse that night. It may even spark a conversation between him and his friends. They may even talk about the online execution and try it out to see how they score on the good taste test later in the week.

Dogs ✓
Tattoos ✓
Tattoos of Dogs ✗

Amstel Pulse. Micro filtered to ensure good taste

IDENTIFYING THE TARGET MARKET FOR THE FIGURE 8 YOGHURT BRIEF

You are about to create a character sketch of the person who is most likely to buy Figure 8 yoghurt for himself. Turn to the template at the back of the book called 'Who Are You?' and either scan the page into your computer, or make a copy so that you can look at each of the three guiding paragraphs as you devise your character.

For the purposes of discussion, let us call the person Mark. (You are free to choose any name you like, but we will work with the name Mark as we develop the brief.)

Concentrate on the aspects of Mark's life relevant to the objective set out in Chapter Two: 'to encourage a man not to resist buying low-fat Figure 8 for himself'.

It's fine to write more than you need. Then go back and trim it to the essentials that define Mark's way of life in relation to why and when he would choose to buy and enjoy Figure 8 on a regular basis. Too much extraneous detail can make this template confusing as a working tool. The Amstel example gives just enough detail to convey a clear idea of the primary target audience.

1. Think of a young man you know who likes yoghurt. (Remember, the objective isn't about persuading someone to like yoghurt.) You can construct a character from a combination of aspects of young men you know. This is how novelists, TV and screenwriters writers work. How confident is Mark? How much does he care about fitness and eating the right thing? Remember that his girlfriend buys Figure 8. Does he like taking advice from someone else? Mark is in a relationship, but he doesn't live with his girlfriend. One key insight here is imagining someone who, once he finds something he likes, even if it's not aimed at him, is confident enough to choose it given the right advertising message.

2. Decide what you want to say to Mark. The right strategy would give Mark 'permission' to buy this for himself. He has to be the kind of guy who has a mind of his own, yet also listens – at least some of the time – to someone he admires and who knows what they are talking about.

3. Imagine Mark's day, what job he might have, what his mornings are like when he's rushing off to work – all of this will give you ideas for the kind of communication that Mark might react to in a positive way. Whatever the media, from apps to a poster, the clearer your picture of Mark, the more likely you are to connect with him.

4. STRATEGY

HOW WILL YOUR ADVERTISING ACHIEVE YOUR TASK?

This section of the brief distils, into one sentence, how your advertising will achieve its task of meeting the agreed objective. Defining the strategy exemplifies a planner's skill – and yours, particularly if you are working freelance or in an agency without planners. There is never just one possible strategy for a particular objective, and it's smart to come up with several viable directions. Of course, once a strategic route has been successful, you can't imagine having done it any other way!

Answering the question 'How will your advertising achieve your task?' is probably the most demanding aspect of constructing a strong creative brief. It also yields the greatest rewards. Good strategies make the difference between forgettable, ineffective advertising, and brand-changing, breakthrough advertising. This section sits at the very heart of the creative brief, informed by the insights of the preceding sections – product/service, objective and target market – and determining the shape of the sections that follow.

The mark of a good strategy lies in its potential to help you make that creative leap into solving your client's problem in fresh, original ways, whatever the media. While a good strategy doesn't guarantee great advertising, a weak strategy almost inevitably leads to conventional, ineffective solutions. Clients and their agencies need to take calculated risks to achieve distinctive strategies so that the advertising can achieve its objective. Strong strategies outlast individual campaigns.

At the time, a proposed strategic route can seem risky, even outlandish! In 1969, it took courage for VW to accept DDB's bold strategy of advertising the Beetle by telling Americans the alarmingly honest truth about the simple, unassuming, reliable car – it's ugly, but it gets you there.

It's ugly, but it gets you there.

This 1969 ad exemplifies DDB's breakthrough strategy for VW, which marked a revolution in American advertising. It shows the ungainly lunar-excursion module, thereby mirroring the VW Beetle's unflashy appearance, while celebrating the first manned moon landing.

DEFINING STRATEGY

Originally a military term, 'strategy' is usually a closely guarded secret, whether it's used in combat, in political elections, or in advertising campaigns for everyday goods and services. The term 'campaign' is also a military term. This battlefield language has been used in advertising for decades. It describes, if not a war zone (fortunately no one gets killed), certainly a landscape with obstacles to overcome.

These obstacles are physical and psychological. Consider the normal landscape within which advertising takes place, in whatever country, whatever medium. There is almost always strong competition in the form of other products and services. At the same time, there are psychological barriers – habits, ingrained attitudes, likes and dislikes, prejudices, indecision, and all the variables of human nature – as well as the sheer overload of communication. All of which together makes it a challenge for your advertising to break through and engage the interest of your primary audience.

IDENTIFYING A 'DISRUPTIVE' STRATEGY

Jean-Marie Dru, chairman of TBWA Worldwide, coined the concept of 'disruption' in advertising. He identified 'disruption' as the shared characteristic of distinctive, brand-changing campaigns, citing examples such as VW, Avis and Apple. When Dru looked at what made these campaigns similar, he saw that the way of thinking always represented a 'before and after'. There was a discontinuity, a breakthrough, a revolution – a 'disruption'. This concept defines and demands unconventional thinking. Just as Bill Bernbach resisted the strategies of mainstream car advertising, instead telling Americans to 'think small', Steve Jobs, head of Apple, originated the notion that a technologically advanced brand 'is not about bytes and boxes, it's about values'. In French, Dru's native language, *une disruption* refers to a sudden opening of an electrical circuit – thus lending a powerful surge of energy to this concept of creating strategies that break through conventional thinking.

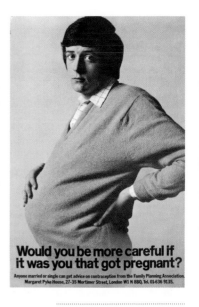

Would you be more careful if it was you that got pregnant?

Anyone married or single can get advice on contraception from the Family Planning Association.
Margaret Pyke House, 27-35 Mortimer Street, London W1 N 8BQ. Tel. 01-636 9135.

This Health Education Council poster from 1969 finds its way through to the individual with an unexpected, yet relevant strategy by challenging the man's eyes and ears, mind and heart. It was created at Cramer Saatchi by copywriter Jeremy Sinclair, art director Bill Atherton and photographer Alan Brooking.

Dru's disruption theory helps you to assess the strength of a strategy, whether you're devising it with a planner or on your own. The thinking behind the Health Education Council poster about contraception shares the disruptive quality common to the classic campaigns Dru discusses. The client set the objective: 'to raise the issue of contraception and encourage young men to take greater responsibility'.

A more conventional strategic approach would have been to focus on a young woman. Instead, the disruption occurs by forcing a young man to face up to what it looks and feels like to be visibly 'in trouble'. As a result of what was a shocking image, attitudes to sex education began to change. Created at Cramer Saatchi in 1969, this poster is widely considered to have marked a sea-change in UK advertising – as revolutionary as Bernbach's work at DDB for Avis and VW – and it was the impetus for the birth of Saatchi & Saatchi.

DISRUPTIVE STRATEGIES CROSS BORDERS

When BBH convinced Levi Strauss that the way forward was to return to their roots, this objective, as we saw in Chapter Two, won them the account. Now a huge task lay ahead for BBH. The company was, in John Hegarty's words, 'still this young upstart agency with everything to prove, especially our ability to come up with an idea that could cross borders and inspire European youth'.

The product was the original 501 button-fly, stone-washed denim jeans. BBH identified that a mass fashion look was taking hold, powered by music. Hegarty decided that the strategy to sell these jeans would be to position them at the 'very heart of youth culture'. However, the jeans were considered expensive, plus research showed that men preferred zips to the old-fashioned button fly. Undaunted, BBH created the brand-changing commercial 'Laundrette', starring Nick Kamen.

By unapologetically concentrating on the product, placing the action in a mythical American time frame, and helped by Kamen's mesmeric performance, these old-fashioned original jeans became the latest must-have thing. The button fly now seemed authentic, provocative. The campaign, which included a second commercial, had to be pulled after only a few weeks. The 501s sold so quickly that stocks ran out, expense somehow no longer an issue. Hegarty notes: 'The lesson for us at BBH was that you could create outstanding, cross-border advertising if you focused on what unites people around a brand, rather than what separates them.'

'Laundrette' was conceived by John Hegarty (art director) and Barbara Nokes (copywriter) and created by Roger Lyons (director). The soundtrack throughout is Marvin Gaye's 'I Heard It Through the Grapevine'.

1   2
        3   4   5
                             6   7
                             8   9

STRATEGIES OUTLAST CAMPAIGNS

A strategy can last for years, whereas the creative work, the campaign that springs from that strategy and expresses the underlying thinking, changes more frequently. Changing fashions in advertising, the appointment of a new brand manager on the client side, a change of agency or budget, a global realignment of the brand, research indicating that the current campaign isn't working, or simply the need to refresh a heavily run campaign – these are all possible reasons for developing new creative work based on the same strategy. Since the strategy can last for a long time, it needs to be clear – especially for a global brand. It forms the bedrock of the brand or service.

1   'Roller Babies' opens with the copy: 'Let's observe the effect of Evian on your body.'

2-6   The lively rap beat and lyrics begin, carrying through to the end. You have to hear the music to appreciate the pace and style.

7   The rap music stops. We hear refreshing drops of water against silence. Translation: 'Drinking a naturally pure, balanced mineral water, maintains the youthfulness of your body.'

9   'Live young.'

'The strategy behind the Evian brand is built on youth, "Live young"', wrote Rémi Babinet, creative director of the Paris advertising agency BETC Euro RSCG. While this strategy hasn't changed in years, its expression – the advertising – has. Evian no longer mentions the Alpine source in its advertising. Instead, it leaves it to the website to support Evian's long-held youth strategy with the details of its source and balanced mineral content. It describes how their mineral water journeys for 15 years 'through an ancient glacial filter deep in the heart of the French Alps', and is bottled at source 'so you can enjoy its naturally pure and refreshing taste anywhere, any time'. Of course, no bottled water can claim to

Boire une eau naturellement pure
et équilibrée en minéraux entretient
la jeunesse de votre corps

evian.
Live young

1 | 2   3
4   5
6   7

make you stay young. But by promising to help your body 'live young', Evian can create many different campaigns.

In the highly competitive bottled-water market, Evian has progressed to a more emotional approach in its advertising, to connect more with its consumers, and has 'moved away from functional messaging', notes Michael Aidan, global brand director for Evian in Paris. Their agency, BETC Euro RSCG, created in 2009 the commercial 'Roller Babies', which is among the most watched ever in online advertising. This has since been followed by their 'T-shirt' commercial, which retains the strategy of 'live young', again showing babies, but in a totally different way.

Roller-skating babies and babies being interviewed were followed by commercials showing vibrant individuals wearing t-shirts with images of babies. The strategy didn't change: suggesting that drinking Evian will help you maintain a youthful body. However, the expression of the strategy moved 'from babies doing stunts' towards a more unified expression of 'you feeling young'. These new executions make the individual become one with the energetic baby. Michael Aidan, quoted above and here from a *New York Times* article (18 April 2011) by Stuart Elliott, crystallized the key executional difference, noting that in these new commercials 'the baby is in you'.

EVIAN'S 'T-SHIRT' INCREASES ITS ENGAGEMENT ONLINE

A strong strategy is single-minded, yet can encompass changes in its expression – in the executions. It might seem as if the 'T-shirt' executions are largely the same as 'Roller Babies'. The difference between them is considerable. The range of people shown, their characteristics, and the lively interaction with each other is far

1   Although this commercial also begins with the copy, 'Let's observe the effect of Evian on your body', this time it appears on someone's body, which gives it a greater impact.

3   'Maintain the youthfulness inside you.'

4–5   Individuals register shock as their bodies appear in the shape of babies.

6   The revelation of the logo and campaign line explain the transformation.

7   'Evian Live Young Make Your Own Film (website)'

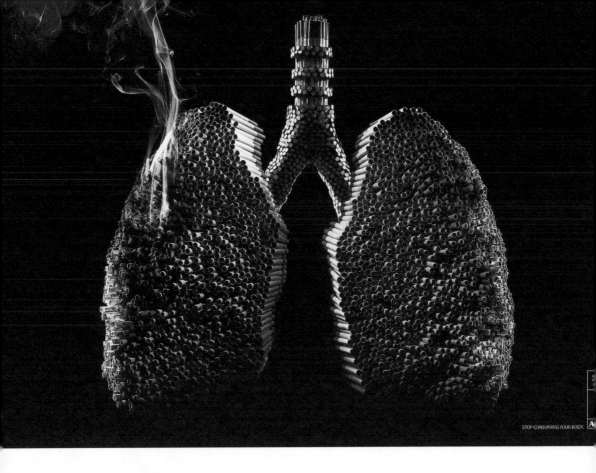

STOP CONSUMING YOUR BODY.

more involving. 'Stunts' can get boring. Had the client insisted on always using real babies, whether or not with CGI, the campaign might not have moved on as successfully. This is a perfect example of staying with the same strong strategy and understanding how the expression of it can change, visually and tonally. The website indicated in the final frame (www.letsbabydance.evian.com) gives viewers a chance to participate in various ways, increasing their engagement with the campaign by adding their own images and creating their own online versions of the commercial.

The strength of this strategic approach works by reminding you that each drag on a cigarette consumes more of your lungs. The burning image stays in your mind, along with the campaign line Stop Consuming Your Body.

HOW TO WRITE A STRATEGY

The strategy describes *how* the objective will be achieved. It is *by means of* a certain action – by suggesting, by encouraging, by demonstrating, by introducing, by resisting, by escaping, by staying, by flying, by walking, by changing, and so on – that a particular strategy will achieve the task in hand. For example, if your objective is to stay fit, one way of achieving that might be: *by cycling to work*.

Tip: Begin your advertising strategy with the word 'by'. If you structure the phrase in this way it distinguishes your objective – in this case, to stay fit – from your strategy. Otherwise, you can end up writing another objective without realizing it.

Here are six more ways, or strategies, to achieve the objective of staying fit. By learning a new sport. By returning to a favourite sport. By eating more sensibly. By joining a yoga class. By joining a gym. By asking a friend to go running with you. Which of these would work best? It depends on who you are, what your life is like.

It also depends on your motivation. Advertising can only go so far. This powerful Brazilian anti-smoking ad (opposite), which we first looked at in Chapter Two, tackles another issue in which motivation is a key factor. The strategy here works by showing how your lungs are turning to ash, gradually being destroyed with each cigarette you smoke. The stark campaign line, 'Stop consuming your body', pulls no punches. It's meant to frighten smokers. Time will tell how many Brazilians make the decision to give up.

THEORIES OF MOTIVATION

The Brazilian 'Burning Lungs' poster more than meets its advertising objective, but will it motivate someone to stop smoking? External factors might need to come into play. Positive peer pressure. The creation of no-smoking areas. Perhaps the birth of a baby, bringing about concern about the effect of contact smoke. The death of a relative or friend. One or all of these might have to occur for the disruptive 'before and after' effect of the advertising to work. To motivate smokers to change their behaviour – not just think about doing so. Would one of these factors be a 'nudge'?

Many theories set out to explain how and why we act the way we do. Beginning with Sigmund Freud's famous question, 'What do women want?', continuing to Abraham Maslow's 'hierarchy of needs' (see overleaf), Malcolm Gladwell's 'blink' theory, and on to Richard Thaler and Cass Sunstein's recent 'nudge' theory, what can you learn to help you better understand human nature? There are no simple answers. Questions remain about what motivates a person to do – or not do – this or that. If you have studied psychology or behavioural economics, you will have explored various theories in depth. Planners often hold degrees in these subjects. Satisfy your curiosity. Have a conversation with them, and learn more. It is always helpful to understand various theories so that you can use aspects of them to devise and then justify aspects of your strategy in the pitch.

NUDGE

The 'nudge' theory draws on research in psychology and economics. In their book, *Nudge: Improving Decisions about Health, Wealth, and Happiness*, Richard Thaler and Cass Sunstein describe two ways in which we think: the 'reflective system' and the 'automatic system'. You can guess that the first is slow and thoughtful; the second, more instinctive. 'Nudge' is about decision-making, and the conclusions are unsurprising. For example, apparently we often don't make very good decisions. The authors argue that we need help to 'nudge' us into making the better choice. For example, companies enrolling us in a pension scheme instead of relying on us to do it ourselves, or shops putting real oranges by the checkout instead of tempting us with chocolate ones.

We are heavily influenced by peer pressure, even when it's not in our interest. We continue to do things – receiving magazines we're not keen on after free trial issues – out of sheer inaction. You could cite the 'nudge' theory to explain why a strategy of persuading two friends to give up smoking at the same time might be a good idea. The 'nudge' theory is perhaps more useful in terms of corroborating your strategy – supporting your views on why you think it will work – rather than helping you actually devise a strategy.

BLINK

Malcolm Gladwell describes his theory of rapid cognition as 'the kind of thinking that happens in a blink of an eye'. He sees it as perfectly rational: 'It's thinking that moves a little faster and operates a little more mysteriously than the kind of deliberate, conscious decision-making that we usually associate with "thinking".' It seems, from Gladwell's theory, that glimpsing an ad for three seconds could motivate a person to act if the strategy relates to their needs or aspirations (www. gladwell.com).

HIERARCHY OF NEEDS

Abraham Maslow studied one per cent of the US college student population to arrive at his 1943 paper 'A Theory of Human Motivation', which he later developed in his book *Motivation and Personality*, published in 1954. Although this theory has been criticized for being both ethnocentric, and highly individualistic, overemphasizing certain aspects of self-actualization above community spirit, Maslow's theory contains many truths about human nature.

Maslow set out his thinking in a triangular diagram that has become very well known. The more basic needs appear at the bottom of the triangle. Until these needs are satisfied, or taken care of, a person cannot focus on the needs higher up the triangle. Try using Maslow's 'hierarchy of needs' as a tool to see where a strategy appears. Let's use Apple as an example. What needs or aspirations does their strategy address? By concentrating on 'values', rather than 'bytes and boxes', as Steve Jobs said, Apple have aimed to satisfy many of the needs detailed in the top three sections of the triangle.

Maslow's triangular 'hierarchy of needs' illustrates how a person can be motivated to focus on higher-level needs only if his or her basic aspects of survival are taken care of.

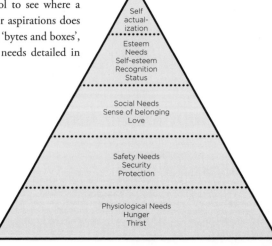

Self actual-ization

Esteem Needs
Self-esteem
Recognition
Status

Social Needs
Sense of belonging
Love

Safety Needs
Security
Protection

Physiological Needs
Hunger
Thirst

This commercial for Marmite by DDB London, 'The Kiss', first ran in 1999. It was directed by Paul Goldman. The Marmite campaign was based on the premise that some people love the product, while others hate it.

1   A couple return to the woman's flat after a date.

2   Woman: 'Coffee?' Man: 'Sure.'

3   Woman goes off to the kitchen.

4   They seem to be getting on brilliantly.

5   The couple begin to kiss.

6   He begins to react badly to a taste in her mouth.

7   He's retching, trying to rid himself of the taste. The woman looks on. She's puzzled, concerned.

8. The product and the campaign campaign line explain the scene in the final shot. The woman has been eating Marmite, which she loves, while making coffee but the man hates the taste.

THE THEORY OF TELLING AN UNVARNISHED TRUTH

Jean-Marie Dru analysed the 'before and after' effect that defines the disruptive energy of breakthrough work. In most cases, the agency overturned conventional thinking. But how? Think back to VW, *The Economist*, Apple, *The Independent*, the Health Education Council's 'Pregnant Man', Levi's, Evian. In each case, the unconventional approach came about perhaps from a knowledge of theory, but definitely by analysing the product, the objective, and the target consumer's relationship with the product. From these insights, each agency developed a distinctive strategy, one that revealed an emotional truth about how a person responded to the product or service, as well as a truth about the product itself.

By admitting the unvarnished truth about consumers' reactions to its taste, Marmite's 'Love it or Hate it' campaign exemplifies disruptive thinking. Marmite, a yeast extract rich in B-vitamins, had perfectly good advertising before this. However, this fearless strategy – by showing that people love it or hate it – propelled Marmite to new levels of popularity. 'Love it or Hate it' chimed with the truth of people's reactions to controversial (and trivial) issues. The phrase entered the language, and over a decade on, this strategy continues. To understand its boldness, consider the initial campaign.

The plotline of this witty commercial from DDB dramatizes Marmite's strategy of showing how people otherwise attracted to each other can also violently disagree! Here, romance vanishes when a passionate kiss carries with it the disagreeable (to him) taste of the Marmite she loves. You can't copy this strategy, but you can learn from the thinking behind it. Always look hard at the truth of a product and the consumer's relation to it – not just those who love it. Then create the best commercial you can.

Further executions of the Marmite campaign took this strategy into a larger arena, from intimate romance to politics. DDB created two spoof party election ads, which appeared online, then on TV, radio, and in the press, slipstreaming into the 2010 UK general election period.

MARMITE AND SOCIAL MEDIA

Marmite made very good use of social media. The fake politicians encouraged the public to vote for them on Facebook. The ads are outrageous and hilarious. Even people who hate Marmite responded enthusiastically to a company brave enough to admit that not everyone loves their brand. To say that this strategy is 'disruptive' is an understatement.

In 'The Hate Party's Stop the Spread', 'politician' Steve Heaving (whose surname is slang for vomiting) delivers his manifesto, calling for Marmite eating zones, and urging for legislation that Marmite eaters be banished to the island of Guernsey. The strategy is fully realized in this commercial, with the positive points of the product cleverly interwoven within Heaving's negative rant.

DEVISING A DISTINCTIVE STRATEGY FOR THE FIGURE 8 BRIEF

This section of your brief answers the question: 'How will your advertising achieve your objective?' You might want to come up with more than one strategy, and then choose the one you think is strongest.

However many different strategies you devise, each has to be relevant to previous sections of your brief so far: the yoghurt itself, the objective, and the primary target audience, characterized by Mark. Your template 'Who Are You?' in the previous chapter has given you a way of thinking about what he is like, how confident he is, how his day goes, how, when and where you might reach him with your message.

Keep that information in front of you as you write your strategies. Look at yoghurt brands to see what they offer. If you don't like yoghurt, talk to a few friends who do. Is it the taste that determines their choice? Range of flavours? Calorie count? All of these? Are they loyal, or do they switch? Answers to these questions could lead to your strategy.

We have said that Figure 8 is low in fat, aimed at women, and comes in good flavours. But that when men are on their own, they don't bother buying any yoghurt even though they like to eat Figure 8 and 'borrow' or 'share' it when they are with their girlfriend (or wife, if you're making the target a married man).

One strategic route to reach Mark could be as follows:

By suggesting to Mark that girls really know about low-fat products.
There's nothing wrong with that, but it's a bit flat. It's true, but it lacks insight. Where does it take you, as far as helping you make the leap to creative solutions? What if you imagine the breakfast that Mark eats when he's on his own. Is it a fry-up which he knows is making him put on weight? Or is it nothing but a cup of coffee, which makes him tired and in a bad mood halfway through the morning because he lacks the healthy protein Figure 8 provides? The answer might give you this, more intrusive strategy, one that might lead to a more creative campaign. Write it on your brief:

By suggesting to Mark that whenever he's on his own, he should breakfast like a woman.

5. PROPOSITION

WHAT'S THE 'HOOK' THAT WILL ATTRACT THE TARGET MARKET?

This section of the brief identifies the most important thing your advertising should convey to the target market. Often referred to as 'the single-minded proposition', it defines what you think will capture, or 'hook', the attention of your primary audience. A proposition has to contain something of value – not to everyone, but to the people you're talking to. What really matters to them about the brand or service? If your proposition can express that, it will give you a springboard for your advertising.

In fact, when you're working on your portfolio, devising your own briefs, a well-written proposition can become your campaign line, perhaps with a few tweaks. That's because both proposition and campaign line express the essence of the brand. Both serve a similar purpose, uniting a variety of advertising executions, and in many instances, a number of product lines, all under a single-minded thought across a multi-channel media landscape, from mobile phones to magazines.

Clearly, the more attractive the proposition, the greater the response. A strong proposition can build a global brand. The global presence of L'Oréal exemplifies how women responded in their millions to the now-famous advertising proposition: 'Because I'm worth it'. This struck a deep chord with women. It boosted their self-esteem, and helped to justify their desire to buy L'Oréal's high-performing, more expensive hair colour. We will explore how this, and other propositions, continue to engage their audiences.

Claudia Schiffer features in the 2011 German TV commercial for L'Oréal's Color Riche lipstick. 'You're worth it', the global campaign line, with slight variations, has attracted women to L'Oréal's many products since 1973.

THE ROLE OF THE PROPOSITION

The role of the proposition is to express in one sentence the essence of what the product or service offers. It should be written in a way that inspires the creative team. Although the strategy is vital, it is 'back room' thinking which consumers don't see. They might guess at the strategy, but it isn't usually visible as a set of words in your resulting advertising. Since the role of the proposition is to convey the main thought that will attract your audience, it addresses that person openly. In marketing speak, it is consumer-facing. That's why it can become your campaign line.

PROPOSITION AS CAMPAIGN LINE

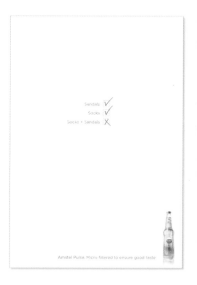

If you're working on your portfolio, using your proposition as your work-in-progress campaign line is an excellent way to develop your campaign. This method keeps your work focused. The proposition, because it expresses the essence of the brand, helps you to underpin the various executions with the main thought as you create ads across various media. You can always shorten, or adjust, the line later. (Note: Of course, when you're working in an agency, whether on placement or in your first job, you will probably receive a brief that is already written. And if your planner has already written the proposition – even if you've helped with it – you will want to come up with a few fresh campaign lines that express that proposition but in your own original ways. Otherwise, your creative director will quite rightly feel that you haven't sufficiently explored new ways of using the language.)

Recall how, in Chapter Three, Ed and Bryan used their proposition for Amstel Pulse as their campaign line: 'Micro filtered to ensure good taste'. The proposition works on two levels – which is of course what makes it such a clever campaign line. Micro-filtering results in good-tasting beer. A good fact. Micro-filtering also helps you distinguish good taste from bad in popular culture. Witty and full of potential for creative executions because of the wider meaning of 'taste'. By using their proposition as a work-in-progress campaign line, they kept their idea on track.

THE PROPOSITION ACTS AS A STIMULUS

A proposition, like a campaign line, should act as a stimulus. If successful, it strikes a chord, relates to a need or desire, perhaps functional, perhaps emotional, probably both, in some combination, which ideally sparks a response from the person you're talking to. A successful proposition engages you – draws you in. There has never been such a thing as a passive consumer. So you should never regard a proposition as merely a statement, or message, which your target audience is expected to swallow and accept, any more than the advertising that you develop from it.

Sender

Receiver

Medium

Stimulus

Response

In order to attract, and engage your audience, your proposition, and the advertising that stems from it, always has to stimulate a response. Keeping this in mind helps you write a better proposition.

HOW THE STIMULUS/RESPONSE WORKS

When you write the proposition, you are addressing a person with the aim of stimulating a response, not just transmitting a 'message'. This stimulus/response process is how creative, effective advertising works, although in more visual and varied ways than the proposition. If you think of a brand as a community, whether national or global, the proposition has to express to thousands, perhaps millions, of people one galvanizing thought that sufficiently sparks their interest to draw each of them to this brand, time and again. It has to have substance, and if it's to last for years, it should be flexible enough to appeal to a changing audience.

L'Oréal's 'Because I'm worth it' achieves that. It has changed over the years to 'You're worth it', and 'We're worth it'. However, the stimulus remains strong. When a woman in their target audience hears that phrase, her response is 'Yes, I guess I am worth it!' Or, perhaps, 'Damn right I am!' – depending on how she feels about herself. 'You're worth it' speaks to a woman in a way that stimulates a response.

Jeremy Bullmore, in his illuminating book *Behind the Scenes in Advertising*, explains the stimulus/response elements in what he refers to as the 'communication

Lego originated in Denmark. 'Lego' comes from the Danish 'leg godt' – 'play well'. This ethos continues to inform Lego's approach. What matters to parents is for their children to use their imagination. In these brilliant German pastiches of changing fashions, sceptical parents styled in the dress of the 1960s, '70s and '80s are introduced by their children to the inventions of the future through the medium of Lego.

chain'. It is often thought that communication is made up of sender, receiver, medium and message. This leads to dull propositions and ineffective advertising because it fails to involve the audience. It merely states the message, without sparking our interest.

Instead, there should be, as Bullmore explains, these five elements: sender, receiver, medium, stimulus and response. The illustrations by Terry Hamaton on the previous page, from Chapter Three of Bullmore's book, show how 'stimulus' and 'response' replace the single element: 'message'. This interplay between your proposition and the audience is key.

NOVELTY AND RESPONSE

One key characteristic of a stimulating proposition is novelty. From early childhood we seem to be programmed to want new things. Gregory Berns, associate professor of psychiatry and biomedical engineering, and author of *Satisfaction: The Science of Finding True Fulfillment*, identifies novelty as the thing that provides the greatest stimulus to the human reward system.

Watching a child play with something new reminds us of how powerful this desire for novelty is. It helps to explain the global success of Lego. Their flagship product, the colourful little bricks, has expanded into an empire of movies, games, video games, and themed amusement parks. In an early campaign, it offered children a true, and irresistible, proposition: 'Lego: A new toy every day'. Children felt rewarded by the act of building a new toy for themselves. The three Lego ads (opposite) capture children's desire for novelty in a more modern way, via their imagination and their vision of the future.

Innovation, especially in consumer-friendly hi-tech products, is moving so fast it's impossible to imagine today what we might want tomorrow. Even as we try to contain our consumerism, a new product comes along so enticing it's hard to resist. Smart phones, satnav, the Kindle, hybrid and electric cars – propositions for these products stir our desire, inviting us to engage with the latest new thing. And millions of us do.

Gregory Berns explains that because 'the world is never stable, never unsurprising ... novelty allows you to build richer models of how everything works'. Berns, who works in the relatively new field of neuroeconomics, says that part of the reason he wrote his book *Satisfaction* 'is to help people, to perhaps help them build a philosophy of what they want out of life. With happiness, it's not like there's an end point – you always adapt. So the key, I think, is to keep trying new things.'

Apple's sleek, design-led products with their intuitive technological features have become as irresistible to teenagers and adults as toys are to children. Even an upgrade, or simply a new colour, such as the white iPhone 4, sparks the desire of Apple's target audience. However, as philosopher Julian Baggini notes, if the object of our desire fails to perform, we soon fall out of love with it. Novelty needs to be underpinned by substance – some kind of support – to maintain our response.

UNEARTHING THE PROPOSITION

Coming up with a good proposition isn't easy, but remember that you're further along than you think. Look again at everything you already know. Deciding what matters most to your potential consumer is based on aspects of the brief you have defined so far: the nature of the product, the objective, the target audience and the strategy. Now put yourself in the consumer's position. What will attract them? What do they care about?

Imagine that you are working at McCann Erickson in New York, and your client is L'Oréal. It's 1973, with women's liberation in full swing. The objective of the brief is to launch Preference, an innovative range of hair colouring. Women have been attracted to L'Oréal's high-performing, scientifically based beauty products since the company began in 1909. But Preference will be the most expensive hair colouring on the market, selling for a dollar more than its competitors. This is the

Finally.

The amazing iPhone, now available in white.

 iPhone 4

challenge that faced Ilon Specht, a 23 year-old woman working on the L'Oréal account at McCann's.

Specht's strategy was to persuade women to buy Preference by justifying its quality. She knew what mattered most to women in this area of beauty. It wasn't saving money. It was about keeping their hair in good condition. Specht defined a proposition that resonated with women, and boosted their self-esteem. She first wrote it in this longer version, from a woman's point of view: 'It's not that I care about money. What matters most is maintaining the good condition of my hair. In fact, it's not really important whether L'Oréal makes me spend more. That's because I'm worth it.' By 1997, the memorable expression extended to all of L'Oréal's products.

'Because I'm worth it', was replaced in the mid-2000s by 'Because you're worth it'. In 2009, it evolved into 'Because we're worth it' to create stronger consumer involvement, following motivation analysis by Russian psychoanalyst Dr Maxim Titorenko.

The Apple iPhone 4 was first launched in black. 'Finally' it appeared in white to tempt the consumer.

'WE DESIRE THINGS THAT WE BELIEVE WILL GIVE US PLEASURE, AND IF WE FIND OUT THEY DON'T, OUR LUST SOON SUBSIDES.'

Julian Baggini

UNEARTHING THE PROPOSITION
INVOLVES LOOKING AHEAD

Everything you have explored so far will help you move towards a proposition. You also will find it useful to bring into the mix two key aspects which form subsequent sections of the creative brief: support and consumer response (see Chapters Six and Ten). By thinking about them now – even though you will address them in more detail later – you will find clues that could help you unearth a few good propositions more quickly.

In these stills from L'Oréal's 2011 German TV ad for Color Riche lipstick, the seductive action of Claudia Schiffer applying the crimson lipstick suggests to women that it could make them look and feel similarly seductive.

LOOK FOR CLUES IN THE 'SUPPORT'

Every proposition you write needs support – a *reason why* the product should interest your target audience. Otherwise, why should they believe you? Once you look at the support, it could become the proposition itself.

Consider the well-known UK campaign for Ronseal, a range of do-it-yourself (DIY) products such as wood stains, varnishes and fillers. Their overall campaign line, stemming from the proposition, is: 'Ronseal. It does exactly what it says on the tin.' The thinking here is that DIY products often let you down – yes, the advertising gives you reasons to believe them – but the products don't work as well as they say they do. Ronseal's proposition counters this by proposing that their products perform exactly the way they're supposed to – just look on the tin.

The proposition in Ronseal's advertisements, enshrined in the phrase, 'Does exactly what it says on the tin', has become part of the language. Because so many things are not believable, from politicians' promises to exaggerated advertising claims, this phrase has become synonymous with believability.

LOOK FOR CLUES IN THE 'CONSUMER RESPONSE'

What do you want the person in your target audience to do, think or feel? Obviously, in the case of Ronseal, you would like the person to buy the product. But before that can happen, the person has to react in a particular way. You want the person to believe that this product works the way the ad says it does. You're on your own, tackling some project which you might not be too good at. In this particular category, DIY, belief in the product is the desired consumer response.

Armed with the knowledge that you can support the proposition with facts about the product, and that the consumer response is what you're looking for, you can develop your proposition. Although these two aspects come later in the brief, they can really help you at this stage. Opposite is the final title frame from a Ronseal TV commercial, which we will look at more fully in Chapter Ten.

PROPOSING THE UNBELIEVABLE

In VW's current UK TV and press advertising, their single-minded proposition is 'Unbelievable value'. Value matters to people. However, it is one of the most overused and, more importantly, unbelievable, propositions. Good value is a phrase used for thousands of products and services in every country. How could

This DDB UK ad expresses a potentially unbelievable proposition – the value of the Golf – with VW's usual wit. By forcing a response of head-shaking disbelief in the actual act of moving your head to read the ad, we believe it. Truly interactive press!

View ANNA monthly press awards at www.the-annas.co.uk

A
is up to
cheaper
run
3
than
competition.
true,
need
shake
head.

Golf
10%
to
over
years
the
It's
no
to
your

Unbelievable value.

Das Auto.

Data supplied by KeeResources Kwik Car Cost June, 2011. Based on a comparison of equivalent models from Honda (Civic i-VTEC SE 5-door 1.4), Vauxhall (Astra Esclusiv 5-door 1.4), Ford (Focus Edge 105 5-door 1.6) and Toyota (Auris Edition 5-door 1.3) to the Volkswagen (Golf S TSI 85 5-door 1.2T). Assumes vehicles cover 36,000 miles over 36 months and cost includes depreciation, fuel costs and road tax over 3 years. For further details on this calculation please search 'Golf 3 year costs' on volkswagen.co.uk. Official fuel consumption in mpg (litres/100km) for the Golf range: urban 23.9 (11.8) – 60.1 (4.7); extra urban 42.2 (6.7) – 83.1 (3.4); combined 33.2 (8.5) – 74.3 (3.8). CO_2 emissions 199-99g/km.

VW venture into this tired territory with any kind of success? Actually, VW has built its brand on the good value it represents. You could say it owns the territory.

In earlier chapters we saw how VW established their brand with Bill Bernbach's groundbreaking strategy: telling the truth about their unassuming, reliable car. It was 'disruptive' advertising, to use Jean-Marie Dru's term for brand-changing advertising. Decades on, DDB continues to advertise VW with single-minded propositions that seamlessly follow the original strategy set in the 1960s.

And because this proposition tackles the word 'unbelievable' along with 'value', it turns ordinary consumer reaction to this kind of promise on its head. Each ad cleverly dramatizes disbelief at VW's competitive value. The proposition, with detailed support, becomes the campaign line, with 'Das Auto' ('the car') as part of the logo.

PROPOSING DEEPLY HELD BELIEFS

The propositions of successful global brands can originate from deeply held beliefs of the company's founder. Discovering, or unearthing, those beliefs reveals the essence of the product or service. If you go on to realize the potential of these beliefs, you can frame a strong proposition that resonates with your audience, and enables you to build the brand, setting that company apart from the competition.

The thinking behind Wieden + Kennedy's global campaign line for Honda, 'The Power of Dreams', stems from Soichiro Honda, the company's founder. He believed we should see the world not as it is, but as it could be. His credo – in Japanese, *Yume no Chikara* – translates as the power of dreams. Dreaming up inventions that shape the future was at the heart of Honda. Soichiro Honda began as a mechanic. A self-taught engineer, he developed a motorized bicycle in petrol-starved post-war Japan by attaching a little motor to a bicycle. Wieden + Kennedy embraced Soichiro Honda's thinking, developed it into their proposition, and began their campaign by asking consumers: 'Do you believe in the power of dreams?'

This proposition was a strong, single-minded thought, but it could have resulted in an ineffective, 'fluffy' campaign. Instead, W+K's strong creative work began with ASIMO, the humanoid robot developed by Honda. And in 2003, The Power of Dreams came into its own with the 120-second TV and cinema ad called 'Cog', created by Matt Gooden and Ben Walker and directed by Antoine Bardou-Jacquet. The brilliantly filmed sequence of 85 individual parts, filmed in one continuous take, creates a precise, mesmerizing, almost playful chain reaction, which results in a car: the Honda Accord.

Because the delicate chain reaction is filmed with no special effects, an astounding feat in itself, it dramatizes the skill of the Honda car maker. There are no digital 'tricks'. With 'Cog', the down-to-earth, mechanical nuts and bolts of car making was transformed. 'Cog' broke through conventional car advertising, expressing the realization of the dream of inventing something new. Honda's target audience responded enthusiastically to the campaign, and especially to 'Cog'. According to Marketing Case Studies, Honda's worldwide sales from 2002 to 2005 rose

1–3   Honda's 'Cog' dramatizes the fusion of imagination and skill required to move into the future, expressing company founder Soichiro Honda's belief in seeing the world not as it is but as it could be.

1
2   3

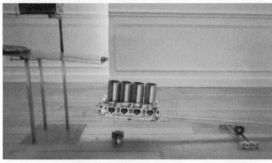 

HONDA
The Power of Dreams

4–10 The movement of the parts is accompanied by subtle sounds of delicately clinking machinery and whooshes of rain.

11   At this point we begin to hear music.

12   Voiceover (provided by writer and broadcaster Garrison Keillor): 'Isn't it nice ...'

13–14 '... when things just work?'

dramatically from 2.6 to 3.2 million units. UK sales went up by 28 per cent. 'Cog' won 37 advertising awards, including an IPA Advertising Effectiveness Award and a Gold Lion at the 2003 Cannes Lions International Festival of Creativity.

In 2011, W+K's launch of Honda's Jazz Hybrid car continued to express Soichiro Honda's belief in innovative ideas that shape the future. The multi-channel, pan-European campaign under the campaign line 'The Power of Dreams' takes the proposition forward in fresh, inventive ways. The flexibility of this campaign line enables W+K to venture into different media with vibrant executions which look very different from 'Cog' yet express the same proposition. We will look at how the multi-channel media campaign works in the final section of the brief.

WRITING A PROPOSITION FOR THE FIGURE 8 BRIEF

Your proposition should be written in one sentence, in a conversational style. A sentence forces you to make it a complete thought, to express your thinking more clearly. You can shorten it later. Since the proposition is an outward expression of aspects of the brief you've already explored, you might have already written the beginnings of several propositions. Look at Chapter Three on Target Market. The template 'Who Are You?' asks you to decide what you want to say to Mark. You should have a sentence prompting Mark to follow his girlfriend/wife's lead and breakfast on Figure 8 yoghurt when he's on his own.

Now have a look at the strategy from Chapter Four: 'by suggesting to Mark that whenever he's on his own, he should breakfast like a woman'. If you turned that strategy around, and addressed Mark, it would say: 'Hey, Mark – why not breakfast like a woman?' What would Mark think of that approach? It could be funny and work well, or it could go very wrong. A lot would depend on the advertising. So it's a possibility. However, it would be good to have another proposition to work with.

We need to get to grips with what matters most to Mark, not just about the yoghurt, but about his breakfast – the 'when' of the product experience, which is also part of the 'Who Are You?' template. Maybe that's where the clue lies to the hook that will attract Mark

to buying Figure 8 on his own. Rory Sutherland believes that the 'when' of your experience with a product very often offers the greatest creative opportunity. Does Figure 8 remind him of having breakfast with his girlfriend/ wife? Perhaps when he's alone, breakfasting on Figure 8 is really satisfying, because of that, not just because it's healthy. What if you proposed something like this to Mark:

Waking up with Figure 8 makes you feel nearly as good as she does.

'Waking up' helps to focus the 'when', and 'feel nearly as good as she does' carries a faint sexual innuendo, but it fails to convince Mark to bother with the yoghurt.

Wake up to what your body wants, every morning. Figure 8.

That's clear, carries a stronger double meaning, and adds 'every morning'. Write it on your brief. You can always shorten the line later, leaving out 'Wake up to'. Also, you can support your ads with facts about how healthy the yoghurt is, and have fun with the creative work.

6. SUPPORT

WHY DOES THE PRODUCT INTEREST THIS TARGET MARKET?

1   2

This section of the brief supplies the justification for your proposition. Good reasons attract your target audience to what you're advertising and offer evidence that the product or service will live up to their expectations. A creative use of these reasons brings your campaign to life. Never think that 'support' refers to a collection of dry facts which you can skate over and get on with the creative work, or you will miss the potential of what can be a goldmine of ideas for your campaigns.

To understand the importance of the support, think like a consumer. You know from your own experience how hollow a campaign can seem when it lacks a good reason to support its claim, especially if you are considering an expensive purchase. If the facts seem either thin or exaggerated and unbelievable, you will probably ignore the advertising and look to the competition. Equally, if the reasons don't support the campaign's main proposition, they won't relate to what you want from the product. An ad filled with extraneous reasons doesn't make it more convincing. For you to respond in a positive way, the support has to speak to what you care about.

How you use the support in your creative work will differ according to what you're advertising, and the medium. You can make it work one way on TV, another in print, yet another way on the product itself. As long as the support relates to your audience, you can use it flexibly to make your point and build a story that attracts your consumer.

BBH's pan-European TV commercial 'Laundrette' for Levi's original 501 jeans (see Chapter Four), dramatizes the old-fashioned button-fly style by focusing on the action of a good-looking man unbuttoning and then taking off his jeans before throwing them in the washing machine. It is one of the authentic features that supports the brand's claim: true-blue American heritage. Filming the sequence in a deliberately provocative way made this feature desirable.

Now imagine that after seeing 'Laundrette' you were one of the thousands who ran out and bought the jeans. Inside your brand-new pair of fashionable 501 Levi's, you would have found a version of the same story, told in quite a factual

1   Actor Nick Kamen's demonstration of the jeans' nostalgic button-fly style as he strips down to his old-fashioned boxer shorts is anything but dull. By concentrating on the product, you can make a creative use of its features to support your proposition – the authenticity of Levi Strauss jeans.

2   You can dramatize the support visually, include it in copy, as well as on the product. As you explore the different ways of using the support, it gives you ideas for additional executions. These jeans are 'riveted', the subject of another award-winning BBH commercial.

way. The story of authenticity is spelled out on a huge label, sewn into every pair. Here, Levi Strauss's riveted denim jeans are described as tough, enduring, 'symbolizing the vitality of the West'. This message works to reinforce the TV commercial, and reassures you each time you pull on your 501s that the brand's image is built on a convincing set of facts.

PLANNERS IDENTIFY KEY REASONS TO BELIEVE

In a good agency, the planner will make sure that you have all the relevant facts to support the strategy and proposition. As in every section of the brief, the planner's skill lies in distilling information. A planner will identify the reason, or reasons, most likely to attract your target audience and provide the most convincing support. Only then can you be expected to make the best creative use of it throughout your work.

If there is one key reason plus several other persuasive reasons, use each additional reason one at a time, throughout your campaign, to accompany the main reason. There might be one overriding reason which forms the core of the campaign.

1   With Aussie products the attraction for the target audience, young women, is the ingredient jojoba seed oil, which features here. Its Australian source also links to the product name. Lively copy, rather than gorgeous hair imagery, separates the brand visually from the competition in the hair-care/shampoo market.

2   The support for this ambitious proposition is convincing: 'the purest for the purists'. Five natural ingredients, shown in a strikingly simple way, emphasize the pure lemon taste.

1

2

Then, of course, you would use it in every execution. In the ad opposite, the one strong reason for buying this hair-care range is its 'extracts of Australian jojoba seed oil'. This core reason plays a major role in the visual and copy of the ad. The benefit to women of Take the Heat is to protect their hair from heat. And who knows more about heat than an Aussie?

The number of reasons that make up the support depends on the nature of the product or service. More is not necessarily better. Being presented with a huge pile of reasons will not help you as a creative team. Nor is it easy for your audience to take in more than a certain amount of information in any one execution.

An excellent example of how to handle a group of reasons convincingly and creatively is the American ad for Häagen-Dazs 'five' lemon ice cream. Even the name 'five' derives from the support. The proposition is expressed by the headline, 'the purest for the purists', supported by five 'reasons': milk, cream, sugar, eggs and lemon. These natural ingredients provide relevant, convincing support. Pristinely photographed against white, the freshly cut lemon sings out. Spare copy echoes the main visual: 'Just five all natural ingredients. Simply perfect.' A whisk, laden with whipped cream, points towards the Häagen-Dazs tub, on which the five ingredients are listed. A tempting spoonful of ice cream tops this beautifully realized ad.

TURN ATTRIBUTES INTO BENEFITS

An attribute is a feature or aspect inherent in a product. The benefit describes how that feature makes the product better in some way for the audience. For example, the five ingredients in Häagen-Dazs 'five' are features. How you dramatize the attributes and benefits depends on your product. The consumer expects this ice cream to be better tasting because of the five pure, natural ingredients. Yet the copy never uses the 'benefit' words, 'better tasting'. Instead, the tempting visual provides a stimulus for the reader to respond and think, 'Mmm! – I bet that ice cream tastes good.'

Turning each feature or aspect into a benefit has several advantages. It helps you to see if it really is a benefit. It helps you to identify whether one benefit stands out. Once you've turned attributes into benefits, it speeds up your creative work. You can just glance at your support and begin to create a series of ads more quickly, using each benefit to talk to the person about the product, instead of just stating facts, which makes for quite dull copy. Because you're focused on the benefit, your creative work will be more effective. As in the Häagen-Dazs example, you don't always have to spell out the benefit. It can be done visually.

In Ed and Bryan's brief for Amstel in Chapter Three, they listed three attributes in their section on support in order of importance, turning each one into its benefit. They made sure that the features would mean something to their target audience.

Rock star.

AmpliTube Fender
$14.99 • Find your perfect sound anytime, anywhere. Plug your guitar into your iPhone and choose from 5 classic amps like the Twin Reverb or 6 stomp boxes including distortion or echo.

Live Nation
Free • Always know when your favorite artists are playing near you. Receive automatic alerts based on the music in your library and buy tickets right in the app.

Hype Machine Radio
$2.99 • The best new music from the world's best music blogs is now streaming right to your phone. Hear something you love? Just tap to instantly download it from iTunes.

Djay
$0.99 • Mix and scratch songs right from your music library. This full-featured DJ system boasts pitch bending, automatic beat-matching and more to help you rock your next party.

Vevo
Free • Check out the latest music videos and timeless classics from the web's largest collection. Watch on your iPhone's stunning Retina display or stream them to your HDTV with AirPlay.

iPhone loves music. With over 425,000 apps, the best phone for apps just keeps getting better.

 iPhone 4

The first one was the springboard for their initial ads. The other two might be useful as support throughout the rest of their campaign. Here are the three:

1.   Filtered – means removing the bad flavours.

2.   Modern, clear glass bottle – so you can see what you are drinking.

3.   Ring-pull bottle opening – means you can drink it anywhere.

CONSUMERS WANT INSTANT BENEFITS

Consumers want to know the benefits instantly. Ads have to catch us on the move. Banner ads flash on and off while our mind is elsewhere. We flick through magazines quickly, giving most ads about three seconds' attention. No one wants to spend his or her time figuring out an ad and guessing what's in it for them. Especially if a product is new, with new features, turn them into benefits to help you understand how best to dramatize them. Then visualize or describe them in a clear, lively way.

This American ad for Apple's iPhone 4 doesn't just state the features of the apps. It describes their benefits to attract the target audience of music-lovers more quickly and convincingly.

Opposite is an American full-page magazine ad for the Apple iPhone 4: 'Rock star'. It highlights five music apps – features, or attributes – from among the iPhone's 425,000 apps (and counting). Accompanying each app icon is a crisp, but comprehensive description of its benefit. Had the creative team simply named the five apps, it would be a far less informative ad, and much less convincing to its music-loving audience. These apps were new at the time of this ad (2011). If the features were familiar you wouldn't need to describe the benefits as fully. Familiar or not, it's always useful to turn every feature into a benefit to help you focus on what a person needs or wants from that feature.

FACTS AND OPINIONS

Support for a proposition can range from fact to opinion. Facts include product features – attributes – such as the Häagen-Dazs ingredients or the iPhone 4's music apps. A product's heritage – as in Levi's original 501 denims, for example – is a fact. Scientific findings that back up claims about product performance, for example in the skin-care category, provide convincing support, and ensure that the advertising claims are legal. Opinion-based support includes celebrity endorsement, testimonials from satisfied customers, and results from accredited consumer and government surveys. You can use a mix of fact and opinion. What works best?

A strong celebrity endorsement can outweigh a list of facts, just as one galvanizing fact can prove far more convincing than glittering praise from a famous person. However, the category within which the product or service sits, tends to be the deciding factor as to what kind of support a person finds attractive and/or convincing.

In the fragrance category, support rarely consists of scientific facts. It might impress a person to learn how thousands of flowers are gathered and then pressed to create an ounce of a particular fragrance. But would that attract anyone enough to rush out and buy it? If, however, a fragrance originates from a fashion house such as Chanel, or is branded by a celebrity, that fragrance is more likely to attract people than if it were supported by any fact.

Celebrities with international appeal are worth millions because they themselves are the compelling reason. The launch ad for the men's fragrance Homme by David Beckham, consists of the 'fact' of him: football superstar, handsome. A global celebrity. David Beckham is the reason to try this new arrival into a highly competitive category.

THE SCIENCE OF SKINCARE

Whereas a celebrity can provide the sole support for a fragrance campaign, the skincare category is a different story. Here, scientific findings play a key advertising role, backing up promises of younger-looking skin for women. Many brands, including Clinique, Dove and L'Oréal, also offer skincare ranges targeted at men. For men and women, science supplies support for product performance, giving the target audience 'permission to believe' the advertising claims. Does each product live up to its promise? To use the 'Ronseal' phrase: does it do what it says on the tin? The claims have to stand up to scrutiny. If a claim is overambitious, or questionable in any way, the competition, or a member of the public, can take up the issue with the Advertising Standards Authority (ASA) in the UK or the Federal Trade Commission (FTC) in the US and the claim is examined.

SCIENCE PLUS CELEBRITY

L'Oréal's advertising across their entire product range, from skincare to hair colourings, combines a scientific approach with high-profile celebrity endorsement. International spokeswomen include Beyoncé Knowles, Penelope Cruz, Jennifer Lopez, Andie MacDowell, Claudia Schiffer and Rachel Weisz. Clearly, women are attracted and convinced by L'Oréal's pairing of opinion and fact: celebrity endorsement and scientific findings. Women are attracted by the celebrity and convinced by the science to try the product. They are then satisfied by the product's performance, which makes them keep on using it. Evidence that this dual approach works can be found in L'Oréal's Plénitude Revitalift anti-wrinkle cream, which leads the world market in this highly competitive category.

L'Oréal has always invested millions on scientific research and development, and has based its advertising on explaining it. In a recent UK commercial for Revitalift, Rachel Weisz says: 'I trust science – not miracles.' Whether women understand the science is not to diminish its value as support. At the launch of Revitalift, the TV commercials visualized how the product worked, to justify its efficacy. L'Oréal's international campaign line, 'You're worth it', further justified women's decisions to purchase.

The stills opposite are from an early (2001) German TV commercial for this cream, in which American actress Andie MacDowell draws her archer's bow, and says her target is 'fewer wrinkles and more firmness'. Few people over 40 could argue with that desire. Her arrow takes us to a series of diagrams explaining how the product's key ingredient, Pro-Retinol A, penetrates 'deep into the skin'.

CONVINCING STATISTICS AND COMPLEX ISSUES

Statistics and complex issues can, for your target audience, be either very convincing and carry immense impact or very tedious and hard to understand, depending on how you handle them in your advertising. If you're not sure what the numbers mean, or what the issue at hand is, always ask. No one minds

1

2   3

4   5

6   7

8   9

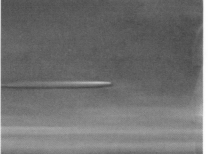

1   Voiceover (Andie MacDowell, dubbed in German): 'My target – fewer wrinkles and more firmness …'

2   '… with Plénitude Revitalift.'

4   Male voiceover: 'Revitalift transports Pro-Retinol A deep into the skin.'

5   'So Revitalift, in less than four weeks …'

6   '… smoothes even deep wrinkles and firms the skin.'

Title: '4 Weeks'

7   Andie MacDowell: 'My target has been achieved!'

8   Male voiceover: 'Revitalift, the anti-wrinkle cream from L'Oréal – evaluated by an independent institute as "Very Good"*.'

Title above the jar: 'L'Oréal: worldwide number one in anti-wrinkle care'

Title beneath the jar: '*Consumer institute: 60 million consumers 4/01'

9   Andie MacDowell: 'Because you're worth it.'

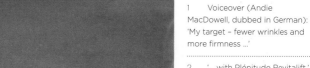

When you have an important issue to communicate, make sure the powerful statistic that supports your story doesn't get lost. By using it as the first line of copy, this surprising statistic grabs your attention and draws the reader into the rest of the copy, which then explains how to avoid this tragic outcome. These terrifying visuals cannot help but stop you, and make you read the alarming statistic, which becomes all too believable when you see all three ads in the campaign (the third is overleaf). It is a stark look at this difficult issue, clearly and sensitively explained. Each ad in this campaign shows an adult curled up in a foetal position (see also following pages), illustrating the potential outcomes of FAS (Foetal Alcohol Syndrome) – adults who grow up to be criminals, as in these ads. By beginning the copy with this alarming statistic, coupled with dramatic visuals, the ads have great impact, and convey the seriousness of the problem.

explaining things and it's essential to feel confident that you know the facts so you can make them clear to someone else.

Your role as a creative is to turn what can look like a lot of undigested numbers and information into a gripping piece of communication. With practice, you learn to 'translate' complex support into a powerful campaign so that when you receive a brief that asks your target audience to commit to something, whether politically or financially, for a charity or any important cause, you will use the statistics and facts in a knowledgeable, convincing way.

The copy in the ad on the left reads: 'Drinking during pregnancy can take years to affect your baby. 50% of children born with foetal alcohol syndrome will grow up to engage in risky sexual behaviour. Do the right thing for your child's sake, don't drink during pregnancy'.

A headline or the first line of copy expressing the essence of a surprising statistic or fact is often the best way into your ad. It gives you a beginning for your argument, and helps you untangle a complex issue into a logical narrative that demands to be read if only for the reader to be satisfied of the truth and importance of this issue.

An effective example of handling a complex issue and alarming statistics is the Foetal Alcohol Syndrome (FAS) campaign in South Africa. Its objective is to raise awareness and challenge misconceptions of this disorder, which is the leading known cause of mental retardation. The Western Cape has the highest incidence of FAS in the world.

'While mothers are aware of the dangers of drinking during pregnancy, most don't realize the long-term risks that even moderate drinking can present for their children,' explains Kirk Gainsford, creative director of the agency Lowe Bull Cape Town which created the campaign in collaboration with the South African National Council on Alcoholism and Drug Dependence (SANCA). Gainsford continues: 'So the primary aim of the campaign was to show what can potentially happen to children of mothers who drink ... effects that can take years to manifest.'

The copy in the ad here reads: 'Drinking during pregnancy can take years to affect your baby. 35% of children born with foetal alcohol syndrome will grow up to abuse drugs and alcohol. Do the right thing for your child's sake, don't drink during pregnancy'.

IDENTIFYING THE SUPPORT FOR THE FIGURE 8 BRIEF

To arrive at the most convincing support, always ask yourself as you're working on a brief: 'why should my audience believe me?' It's another way to frame the question we started with at the beginning of this chapter: why does the product interest this target market? A good idea whenever you're working on a product is to have it on your desk – or at least a photo of it, with the label, so you can see exactly what the consumer sees. Mark might not have ever looked at a yoghurt label. But he will do, once you begin advertising to him in a way that encourages him to think about the category.

We know that Mark is likely to skip breakfast when he's on his own, and just grab a coffee on his way out of the door. Halfway through the morning he feels tired. He'd like to feel as good as he does on the mornings when he has Figure 8 when he is with his partner.

So the support has to include a key ingredient of the yoghurt that will convince Mark that he'll feel more energetic and support the proposition that we arrived at in our previous chapter: 'Wake up to what your body wants, every morning. Figure 8.'

The ingredients in most yoghurts are protein, carbohydrates, fat and salt. Which of these would give Mark an energy boost that will last until lunchtime? Research reveals the answer:

protein. Carbohydrates will give him a burst of energy, but since most yoghurts consist of simple, rather than complex carbohydrates, the burst is short-lived. If you want to explain this difference, you need to understand it, so always do your research to feel confident that you know what you're talking about.

Protein is the key ingredient. That's the main attribute of Figure 8. When you turn it into a benefit, it is: sustained energy for Mark. How much protein does a normal little pot of yoghurt contain? Since this is an imaginary product, we can say that a 120g pot of Figure 8 contains 5g of protein. And how much protein does Mark need? According to the Recommended Nutrient Intake (RNI), a man between 19 and 49 years old needs 55.5g of protein.

So a pot of Figure 8 would be a good kick-start to Mark's day. He could even have two pots, maybe one at breakfast and one mid-morning at work, since the calorie count is quite low: 118 calories. The guideline for his total intake is 2,000 calories a day.

7. COMPETITION

WHO ELSE IS FIGHTING FOR YOUR TARGET MARKET'S
ATTENTION IN THIS AREA?

Avis is only No.2 in rent a cars. So why go with us?

We try harder.
(When you're not the biggest, you have to.)

We just can't afford dirty ash-trays. Or half-empty gas tanks. Or worn wipers. Or unwashed cars. Or low tires. Or anything less than seat-adjusters that adjust. Heaters that heat. Defrost-ers that defrost.

Obviously, the thing we try hardest for is just to be nice. To start you out right with a new car, like a lively, super-torque Ford, and a pleasant smile. To know, say, where you get a good pastrami sandwich in Duluth. Why?

Because we can't afford to take you for granted.

Go with us next time.

The line at our counter is shorter.

No. 2ism. The Avis Manifesto.

We are in the rent a car business, playing second fiddle to a giant.

Above all, we've had to learn how to stay alive.

In the struggle, we've also learned the basic difference between the No.1's and No. 2's of the world.

The No.1 attitude is: "Don't do the wrong thing. Don't make mistakes and you'll be O.K."

The No. 2 attitude is: "Do the right thing. Look for new ways. Try harder."

No. 2ism is the Avis doctrine. And it works.

The Avis customer rents a clean, new Opel Rekord, with wipers wiping, ashtrays empty, gas tank full, from an Avis girl with smile firmly in place.

And Avis itself has come out of the red into the black. Avis didn't invent No. 2ism. Anyone is free to use it.

No. 2's of the world, arise!

1

2

This section of the creative brief puts into focus what is currently going on in the category, so that you can create advertising that is different from it. Although you will have already explored this when developing your strategy, this section reminds you to examine the competitors' creative approaches, as well as their strategies. You wouldn't want to repeat the look and feel of a competitor's campaign, successful or not, simply through not knowing about it. Apart from avoiding what would be an unfortunate oversight, you can learn a great deal from the competition's approach. Their advertising is trying as hard as yours will be to attract a person's flickering attention.

Your creative work needs to stand out. Information on the competition provided by the planner helps you achieve that, but do your own research as well. Trawl the media for competitors' ads. Analyse them. If the category is new to you, explore what kind of communication your intended consumers are seeing, hearing, responding to – or, perhaps, ignoring. Know what your audience responds to before you begin creating your own way of communicating to them. Imagine yourself as part of your audience. It will help you develop an understanding of how people feel about the particular category you're working in – the products or services as well as the ads.

If you're working within a familiar category, you might be the primary audience. That means you will already know the competitors' products as well as their advertising, because it is aimed at you. Yet you might never have analysed it until now. Ask yourself: are all the ads in this category in one tone of voice – either all serious, or all funny? Do they stick to the same medium? TV, posters, digital? Does the leading brand feature celebrities, or ordinary consumers? No people at all? Do the ads have long copy, or hardly any? However you ultimately decide to

1   Bill Bernbach's brilliant insight is that being number two means a company has to 'try harder'. The Avis campaign promises customers a better service than the leader.

2   DDB researched this controversial campaign before showing it to the client. According to Bob Levenson, who later wrote a book on DDB's campaigns, half the people didn't like it. 'But half the people did,' Bernbach said, 'and that's the half we want. Let's go with it.' He was right.

execute your campaign, keep aware of what you are competing with, both strategically and creatively.

Clients are sometimes tempted to ask their agency to follow in the direction of a successful campaign. Mimicking another campaign merely reminds your audience of the other, successful brand. You have to strike out into new territory. How you do it depends on having a distinctive, 'disruptive' strategy. You also have to execute that strategy in creative ways that distinguish your advertising from the competition. This is important whether you're advertising the leader, or a brand that's number two.

SQUARING UP TO THE LEADER

The American campaign for Avis rental cars is a successful example of openly squaring up to the leader. The tiny new Avis company admitted to being number two against the category's famous 'giant' number one, Hertz. This risky strategy worked because it didn't just state that Avis was number two. Every ad in the now-famous campaign makes the point that *because* Avis is number two, 'we try harder'. Created in the early 1960s by Bill Bernbach at DDB NY, the campaign broke new ground in a country where no one wanted to be thought of as second best. The executional style was also distinctive. No car visuals. Just well-written copy, in a friendly tone of voice.

1   2 | 3   4
                    5   6

COMPETE BY TELLING YOUR BRAND'S STORY

Whatever the category, telling the brand's unique 'story' is one way of distinguishing it from the competition. Whereas a particular feature of a brand can be new for a few months, and then be copied by your competitor, a brand's story, if it is distinctive, is impossible to steal. And consumers respond increasingly to the personality which the story creates for the brand. We've seen how this story can come from a brand's origins, as with Evian's Alpine source; from its founder's beliefs, as with Soichiro Honda's credo, 'the power of dreams'; or from a company's attitude and approach, as with L'Oréal, who established early on that women would pay more for scientifically researched, high-performing products, 'Because we're worth it.'

For example, in the bottled-water category, with thousands of brands competing worldwide, each one comes from a source that the consumer wants to believe is pristine. Although each brand's mineral content varies according to its origins, consumers choose more on the basis of taste, price, availability and, importantly, their emotional response to how the brand presents itself. So in the case of mineral water, the story is often about the source of the water, its 'provenance' – where it comes from, and what that particular region imparts to the product's personality.

The advertising for the American brand Arrowhead Mountain Spring Water reveals a story of provenance – the sources of its naturally occurring minerals. Arrowhead originates from several mountain springs throughout the state of California and, at the time of writing, it is the second largest selling brand in the US.

Arrowhead is within the Nestlé company's umbrella of brands, which also includes the US market leader, Poland Spring. Poland Spring's source is in Maine, on America's east coast. Arrowhead and Poland Spring run the same commercial, with only a slight variation in copy, and of course the individual brand shown in the final frames. 'Born Better' is the campaign line for both. Since America stretches 3,000 miles from west to east coast, and these two Nestlé brands are sold

1–2   Male voiceover: 'There are over 358 million trillion gallons of water on earth.'

3   'But not *all* water is created equal.'

4   'Only one billionth of 1 per cent is filtered naturally beneath the earth with the distinct balance of minerals ...'

5   '... and emerges crisp and refreshing enough, to be called Arrowhead.'

6   'Arrowhead 100 per cent Mountain Spring Water. Born Better.'

in different states, viewers only ever see the one commercial. In any case, the sweeping vistas of sky, land and water evoke America's natural beauty. Beautifully shot, the twin ads have a certain epic grandeur in their admittedly traditional approach, which conveys the two stories, one for the brand leader, Poland Spring, and the other for its closest rival, also from Nestlé, Arrowhead.

BRAND LEADERS CAN MAKE THE BREAK

What if everyone's story in a particular category begins to look too similar? Brand leaders can make the break because they have established their story so well. We saw in Chapter Four on Strategy how Evian, after years of featuring its story of Alpine origins, moved to a more emotional, immensely popular campaign, 'Roller Babies', and then to the more personalized expression of its 'Live Young' campaign with people sporting T-shirts with images of babies which interacted with each other. Evian's Alpine origins remain a defining element of the brand's story but no longer need to be expressed in the advertising. So if your brief is to advertise a brand leader, you can make the break, away from the competition, and stay ahead.

In spring 2009, Highland Spring radically changed its advertising from imagery based on its pure Scottish source to a campaign called 'Iconic Love'. It is the UK's leading British-sourced mineral water (second overall in the UK to Evian), and it is also the leader in the sparkling-water category. It is in quite a powerful position. Highland Spring is drawn from protected underground springs in the beautiful Ochil Hills of Perthshire in Scotland. This area has organic status: according to the company website, 'we believe this means our water is as pure as can be'. Like Evian, Highland Spring is a balanced mineral water, very low in sodium and nitrates, which is what you want, and with a clean, crisp taste. A few years ago, the company asked itself, how do we stand out from the competition when sources of water can look so similar? The aim of the campaign 'Iconic Love', a witty, emotional approach, was to associate the brand with the idea of 'unconditional giving'.

Sally Stanley, Highland Spring's group marketing director, explained the reasoning behind this new approach (*The Guardian*, 19 May 2009): 'From an advertising point of view, the bottled-water category is quite predictable at the moment, with one or two exceptions – we've seen mountains, Alps and the like, we don't need to remind people of provenance all the time. ... The difficulty is that although we are the number-two brand in the market we have a lower [ad] spend than our rivals. To get the most return on our ad campaign and engage consumers we have gone for a more emotional positioning.'

The visuals are taken from classic films of the 1930s and '40s. Each ad captures a moment of unbridled generosity as Highland Spring, refreshingly bright green against the black-and-white background, is offered to a companion. The logo reminds us of the water's origins: 'The water from organic land'. The headline reads: 'Now, that's true love'. Two of the four ads are shown opposite: Lassie brings Highland Spring to Roddie McDowall, in a tender moment from *Lassie Come Home*; and Tarzan offers a bottle to Cheetah, in an intimate scene from *Tarzan's Revenge*.

1   Lassie brings a bottle of Highland Spring to a young Roddy McDowall. Although this campaign breaks away from traditional visuals to create an emotional bond with the consumer, the logo reminds us of Highland Spring's purity: 'The water from organic land'.

2   Tarzan offers Cheetah the chimp a generous-sized bottle of Highland Spring. This beautifully art-directed campaign followed one that emphasized a 'reassuringly pure' message in its ads. This very different approach shows the confidence of a leading brand that people trust.

1
2

Wet food is 80% water.
I prefer my food not swimming in water.

Gram for gram, Iams dry food has more high-quality nutrition cats need. As well as more protein, PreBiotics, and vitamins to keep my cat in tip-top condition.

I am more than just a cat.
I am an IAMS cat.

*Vs wet food. Always ensure fresh water is available.

The headline in this poster for Iams dry cat food encapsulates a competitive stance against wet food in a surprising statistic – 80 per cent of wet food is water. The copy spells out the effectiveness, in terms of nutrition, of the ingredients in Iams dry food.

COMPETE WITH CONVINCING FACTS

A fast-growing and highly competitive market is pet food. Here, the target audience is the pet owner, but the 'consumer' is, of course, the pet. Ultimately, whatever the advertising promises, if the dog or cat doesn't like the food the owner will switch brands. Cats are notoriously choosy about their food, far more so than dogs.

The pan-European brand Iams uses a mock-testimonial approach – the 'voice' of their TV and print advertising is from the cat's point of view. This kind of execution – using the pet's point of view – is not new. What this ad successfully does is to separate Iams from 'ordinary' cat food, by taking on the category of ordinary 'wet' food, giving Iams a superior position in a market where owners want to do the best for their pet. (There is ongoing debate in cat owners' forums about which is better – wet or dry food. Iams sells both. However, in its advertising Iams claims that its wet-food products are not 'swimming in water', as referred to here in a disparaging way by the Iams cat. The Iams wet-food variety is described as gravy-based and just as nutritious as the dry-food equivalent. The Iams cat states that ordinary wet foods are 80 per cent water and less nutritious than dry food.)

COMPETING AGAINST A STATE OF MIND

In certain categories your competition is the target market's state of mind rather than another product or service. Here are some examples: complacency (failing to switch to a cheaper tariff, in spite of online comparison websites); apathy (not bothering to vote); irresponsibility (fear of ruining a romantic moment outweighing consideration of the consequences of unprotected sex). These are all powerful states of mind that issue-based advertising campaigns address.

Charities compete with each other for people's generosity but it's really an attitude you are up against more than the competition of one charity against another. Many people feel what is called 'donor fatigue', simply from receiving so many requests from so many good causes. Charities need to generate money to help solve the desperate problems their work is addressing. Most people, if asked, would like to support several charities. However, tight household budgets make it difficult to give even small amounts, however well-intentioned a person is. Some think their contribution will be too small to make a difference, and give nothing at all. How do you make someone feel the immediacy of the need, and the value of their contribution, however small?

We saw in Chapter Two how the Spanish commercial 'Team Hoyt' for the Spinal Cord and Brain Injury Telethon had as its aim to convince viewers about the importance of their donations to the fight against spinal cord and brain injuries. This insight into what could make a viewer donate money led to a moving commercial and a successful outcome in terms of donations.

Following the global economic meltdown of 2008, the UK charity Shelter recognized that the already serious problem of homelessness was about to get even worse. Adam Sampson, then chief executive of Shelter, said: 'With more than 1.9 million households on council-housing waiting lists in the UK, we can no longer stand back and watch our housing market collapse.' Shelter launched, through the Leo Burnett agency, an arresting and penetrating advertising campaign called 'House of Cards'.

This universal metaphor for the fragility of one's house made an immediate impression as people saw the startling images on posters and TV. Five hundred posters appeared in underground stations all over London. Sampson noted: 'Our new "House of Cards" campaign aims not only to wake people up to the fact we are in the midst of a huge housing crisis in the UK, but also to remind people that Shelter is here to help anyone at risk of losing their home.'

Would you be more careful if it was you that got pregnant?

Anyone married or single can get advice on contraception from the Family Planning Association. Margaret Pyke House, 27-35 Mortimer Street, London W1 N 8BQ. Tel. 01-636 9135.

The competition for your audience's attention may be a state of mind, rather than another product or service. Here, the attitude of the young man could be fear of ruining the moment.

1   2 | 3

1   The challenge for advertising in the charity sector is greater than ever. The highly successful 'House of Cards' campaign from Leo Burnett, created by writer Pete Gosselin and art director Jay Hunt, touched people at a time when no one felt safe economically. It brought in hundreds of thousands of pounds in donations and continues to be the backbone of Shelter's advertising.

2   These posters were accompanied by a TV commercial with a voiceover by actress Samantha Morton, who experienced homelessness herself as a child: 'I know how hard it can be. That's why I am supporting Shelter's new "House of Cards" ad campaign and I hope it has the impact needed to help people who are homeless or trapped in bad housing right now.'

3   The striking metaphor of fragility in the 'House of Cards' visuals, accompanied by stark facts on each poster, make this campaign a powerful tool for raising awareness of the problem of homelessness and attracting donations for Shelter.

Today, over 200 homes will be repossessed.

Please help at shelter.org.uk/cards

Shelter
The housing crisis is real

Think about the wider context within which your advertising will appear. The person you are talking to has a life. Always remember that your momentary communication, however strong, will be fighting for attention along with a million other things that person is thinking about, and, at that particular moment, worrying about. The Shelter campaign's insight was that the image of a house of cards spoke to everyone at that moment. No one felt safe, even if they had a job and a perfectly sound roof over their head, because the financial world was out of control. It hit home, so to speak. The poster and TV campaign helped to raise awareness and money for the charity. Note how each poster reveals another shocking fact about the housing crisis, which, worryingly enough, showed a few years on, in 2011, a worsening of 10 per cent on the previous year.

A GOOD WEBSITE MAKES IT EASIER TO GIVE

The Shelter website www.shelter.org.uk/cards (see below) is clear, compelling and consistent with the advertising campaign. It's an excellent example of staying on strategy throughout the media mix, and making sure that the story continues from poster to TV to online, using each medium to its best advantage. In a competitive area such as charity donations, it's particularly important that there is a seamless strategic approach with a simple mechanism for a person to respond quickly and positively to your message.

WHO OR WHAT IS <u>COMPETING</u> WITH FIGURE 8 YOGHURT FOR MARK'S ATTENTION?

To work on this section of the brief in particular, you have to visit a good-sized supermarket and explore the yoghurt section. You will see that the huge choice facing someone like Mark, who is new to the category, could be quite bewildering.

Until Mark became interested in yoghurt, he never realized how many different products there were to choose from. Global brands such as Danone and Nestlé each offer a wide range of choices. According to where you live, there are many smaller dairies, some of which make yoghurts from sheep's milk or goat's milk, as opposed to the vast majority of bigger brands which are made from cow's milk.

The yoghurt market keeps expanding, from plain to flavoured, to ultra-creamy ones that are really more of a dessert than a breakfast food.

In the last chapter we identified protein as the main support, or attribute, of Figure 8. Its benefit, sustained energy, is what will give Mark reason to believe that this is the one for him. You could create a campaign that said Figure 8 has 5g of protein per 120g pot. Would Mark bother to check whether he could get more protein from another yoghurt? In fact, goat's milk yoghurt contains more protein than yoghurt made with cow's milk. However, Mark isn't very experimental and doesn't even want to try that variety. Still, it's

important that you know that fact, so that you don't make a wild claim that is untrue. You always need to know what the competition is.

Given that Mark has already tried Figure 8 and likes it, the competition isn't going to be another yoghurt with only slightly more protein than Figure 8. You need to reassure Mark that Figure 8 has one of the highest levels of protein he can get, but you don't need to enter into tiny details. Those amounts might change, and then you would lose Mark's confidence in your advertising.

The competition for Mark's attention might be his own apathy. He simply can't be bothered to remember to buy yoghurt for himself for the days when he's waking up on his own. So it's an attitude that is the main competition, rather than another product. This insight will give you an idea for how and where to advertise Figure 8 to Mark. You will want to include the very important fact of protein giving Mark sustained energy but not in a way that goes head to head with another product in the category.

Apathy is what prevents Mark from buying Figure 8 for himself, so write that on your brief.

8. MANDATORY ELEMENTS

WHAT HAS TO APPEAR IN THE ADVERTISING
– E.G. A LEGAL REQUIREMENT

This section of the brief describes what you have to include in your advertising, whether it is a legal requirement, or something the client expects to see. The mandatory section also describes what cannot be in your advertising – again, either for legal reasons, or perhaps because of research findings that indicate it's wise to steer clear of certain language or imagery. Even if this section contains only a few words, don't overlook its importance to your creative work. Sometimes a precise stipulation can even give you an idea for your campaign, because it sets your mind thinking about what you can and cannot include. Perhaps the client demands that your ad includes a sizeable logo. If the client is adamant about its size, you might have to create the ad around the logo. Who knows? It could be a brilliant solution.

While you cannot argue with legal guidelines, you can usually discuss a client's demands, or expectations, and sometimes win them over. A common mandatory is to include the product. Let's say that the agency agrees to that. As you develop your creative work, you realize that your idea depends on *not* showing the product.

Take another look at BBH's initial ad for Levi Strauss to launch their black denim jeans. When the fledgling agency presented the visual of a flock of white sheep all going one way, contrasting with a black sheep heading in the opposite direction, the client was understandably surprised to see that no jeans featured in the execution! John Hegarty recalls: 'We argued that everyone knew what a pair of jeans looked like: we had to dramatize black and its value.' Had the client insisted on showing the product, this iconic start to the Levi's campaign might never have seen the light of day. Of course, it helps if your solution is as inventive as this.

This is an uncluttered, effective and creative solution, thanks to a brief that did not contain unnecessary mandatory elements. It invites people to celebrate the London Eye's 10th birthday, offering them a 10 per cent discount on their ride and directing them to the website.

KEEP MANDATORY ELEMENTS TO A MINIMUM

Imagine that you are given a brief that has as its objective to celebrate the tenth anniversary of the London Eye (see previous page). There are four mandatory requirements: show the London Eye; mention a 10 per cent discount offer; include the website address; and display the logo. There is no mandatory requirement to show someone enjoying the ride. That means your creative options are open. You can consider including a close-up of one of the pods, as well as the whole wheel, but you don't have to go down that route. If showing someone enjoying the ride were one of the mandatory elements, you would have to consider how to keep the ad uncluttered yet include a child, or a family group, perhaps a couple – reacting with pleasure at the view from the London Eye. Fortunately, all you have to do is show the wheel.

This ad makes the most of the tenth anniversary by using the wheel itself to depict the zero. It would be far less effective had there been a mandatory requirement to include people, so if you think a mandatory element might be too restricting have a word with your planner. Less is more.

LEGAL MANDATORIES

If you are working on alcoholic drinks, food, cosmetics, financial services, pharmaceuticals or products aimed at children, your brief will include certain legal requirements. Don't worry. Your agency will steer you through the approval process so that your creative work complies with them. Rules and how they are regulated vary according to the country, and the product or service category. Since it would take a book in itself to list all the rules, what follows is a snapshot of the most stringently regulated category and territory: alcoholic drinks in the US, UK and Europe.

To give you an idea of how to handle the key mandatory issues when creating your ads, keep in mind these three rules common to every country in which alcohol advertising is allowed: advertising should not be designed to appeal to people under the legal drinking age; it cannot promote brands based on alcohol content or its effects; it cannot encourage irresponsible drinking.

In the US, as in the UK and Europe, the advertising industry has set up its own regulatory body, which has drawn up the standards for the ethical advertising of alcohol. Although there is criticism that marketing and advertising tactics still attract a younger audience, for the most part, because of generally strong self-regulation, alcohol advertising has mostly avoided intervention by the government. It is in the interests of clients and their agencies to act responsibly so that they can continue marketing and advertising without giving rise to stricter government legislation or attracting endless consumer complaints. Currently in the US, alcohol advertisements can only be placed in media where 70 per cent of the

A TOAST

TO NEAREST
TO DEAREST
TO THE CREW
TO CAHOOTS
TO THE ONES WHO'VE BEEN THERE
TO THE ONES WHO'LL BE THERE
TO DROPPING EVERYTHING
TO SAYING ANYTHING
TO NO JUDGEMENTS
TO NO DOUBTS
TO LOYALTY
TO TRUST
TO FAVORS
TO LIFELONGS
TO BEEN TOO LONG
TO NOTHING'S CHANGED
TO HAVING HISTORY
TO HAVING YOUR BACK
TO MOVING AWAY
TO NEVER TOO FAR
TO GROWING UP
TO SETTLING DOWN
TO YOUR SECOND FAMILY
TO FRIENDS

TO CELEBRATING THE HOLIDAYS
WITH THOSE WHO MATTER MOST

GREY GOOSE
World's Best Tasting Vodka

audience is over the legal drinking age. The decision to accept an individual ad or a category of advertising is always at the discretion of the particular media owner or publisher.

Certain creative devices, such as using cartoon characters as spokespeople, is discouraged. Most spirits advertising carries the phrase: 'Please Drink Responsibly', or 'Sip Responsibly', or 'Sip Slowly'. Responsibility is at the heart of the message. There are also mandatory visual considerations. The American magazine ad for Grey Goose (above) shows how creative work meets the US guidelines, visually and in terms of language: the overall concept of the ad is celebration. It invites you, the reader, to raise a toast to the many reasons why you feel the way you do about the people 'who matter most'. The mandatory phrase, 'Sip Responsibly', appears in small but readable type (bottom right) on the left-hand page. Implicit in the word 'sip' is that one should savour a drink, rather than guzzle down several in a row without taking time to pause between 'sips' to enjoy the occasion.

We see two cocktail glasses, not one. This follows US and EU guidelines to avoid implying that a person is drinking alone. The list on the right-hand page includes significant and seemingly insignificant reasons to celebrate, all of which adds up to a feeling that taking care of your family, friends, and yourself, matters. This reinforces the message of enjoying a drink with a sense of responsibility – the main thrust of the guidelines. The campaign line, 'To living in good company', underlines this thought.

The concept of this celebratory US ad for Grey Goose vodka is about spending time with the people who matter most to you. This premium vodka strikes the right note within a sector whose mandatory guidelines encourage a responsible attitude towards drinking.

WHO MAKES THE RULES?

In the UK, as in the whole of the EU, the advertising industry is self-regulatory, based on a system agreed by the clients, their agencies and the media owners. Each agrees to uphold high standards in advertising; to ensure that ads are legal, decent, honest and truthful. As in the US, it is in everyone's interests for the system to work. But just because it's self-regulatory doesn't mean that it's voluntary. There are rules.

In 2005, the European Union and the United Nations' World Health Organization (WHO) developed a policy for the region which set out basic principles including this underlying ethical belief: 'All children and adolescents have the right to grow up in an environment protected from the negative consequences of alcohol consumption and, to the [greatest] extent possible, from the promotion of alcoholic beverages.'

Restrictions were already in place from 1989 to cover cross-border TV advertising, and were updated with new legislation in 2006/7 to include digital advertising. They were further revised in 2011 to include all websites, as well as ads on mobile phones – whatever constitutes advertising. This 'Audiovisual Directive' makes it clear what alcohol advertising cannot do:

- it may not be aimed specifically at minors, or, in particular, depict minors consuming these beverages;

- it shall not link the consumption of alcohol to enhanced physical performance or to driving;

- it shall not create the impression that the consumption of alcohol contributes towards social or sexual success;

- it shall not claim that alcohol has therapeutic qualities or that it is a stimulant, a sedative or a means of resolving personal conflicts;

- it shall not encourage immoderate consumption of alcohol or present abstinence or moderation in a negative light;

- it shall not place emphasis on high alcoholic content as being a positive quality of the beverages.

In addition to these EU directives, the UK has specific rules, which have been written by two industry bodies: the Committee for Advertising Practice (CAP) for non-broadcast advertising; and its sister organization the Broadcast Committee of Advertising Practice (BCAP) for broadcast advertising. The rules, which are called advertising codes, cover the media spectrum: from print to posters, direct mail, TV, radio, internet advertising, marketing communications on companies' own websites, cinema and promotions.

A planner will summarize the relevant rules and guidelines in the mandatory section. However, it is useful to do your own research and read the rules for yourself. First-hand knowledge of what your client's business is up against makes you a stronger creative, more confident in a meeting, and enables you to create the most effective advertising without breaking the rules. For example, the last sentence in the UK rules below, referring to soft drinks used as mixers, is very interesting – something you might not know about if you were working freelance, and to a tight deadline. Here is the section on alcohol from CAP and BCAP's informative website, www.cap.org.uk. You can see how it reflects the EU-wide rules, and how the thrust of the mandatory issues on alcohol advertising revolve around targeting over-18 year olds and encouraging responsible drinking.

Broadcast Committee of Advertising Practice Code, Section 29: Alcohol

- Principle
  Advertisements for alcoholic drinks should not be targeted at people under 18 years of age and should not imply, condone or encourage immoderate, irresponsible or anti-social drinking.

- The spirit as well as the letter of the rules in this section applies.

- Definitions
  The rules in this section apply to advertisements for alcoholic drinks and advertisements that feature or refer to alcoholic drinks. Alcoholic drinks are defined as those containing at least 0.5 per cent alcohol; for the purposes of this Code low-alcohol drinks are defined as drinks containing between 0.5 per cent and 1.2 per cent alcohol.

- Where stated, exceptions are made for low-alcohol drinks. But, if an advertisement for a low-alcohol drink could be considered to promote a stronger alcoholic drink or if the low alcohol content of a drink is not stated clearly in the advertisement, all the rules in this section apply. If a soft drink is promoted as a mixer, the rules in this section apply in full.

WHO ADMINISTERS THE RULES?

In the UK, the Advertising Standards Authority (ASA) is the independent body that administers the rules and investigates any complaints. Complaints can come from the public, or a competitor client or agency. The rules are strictly enforced: remember, the system is self-regulatory but not voluntary. You have to adhere to the rules. As Louisa Bolch, an ASA council member, explained in a recent interview in *The Independent Magazine*:

'The ASA judges adverts that are complained about against the industry's codes and works out whether the advert needs to be withdrawn or whether it's OK. We uphold complaints on about 2,500 adverts a year and there are millions, so it's important to get a bit of perspective – that's a tiny, tiny proportion.'

She went on to say: 'We don't withdraw adverts lightly; it's a serious business.' Bolch makes the distinction between complaints that have to do with a false claim, and those that have to do with the more difficult areas – issues of taste and decency. 'If an advert says "this product can do x and this product can't do x", that's really straightforward. More interesting is the stuff around taste and decency, and harm and offence. We ask, is this something the majority are going to find offensive?'

The ASA runs ads to inform the public of its work, with its website address (www.asa.org.uk) and a contact number to ring if you have a complaint. It's well worth looking at the website, which is regularly updated with 'hot topics'. You can find advice on issues you're not sure about when creating your ads – especially helpful when working freelance.

RESPONSIBILITY
AND PERSONALITY

It may well be that navigating the rules and guidelines within this category has encouraged an unusually high degree of creativity across the category. UK beer advertising in particular has created distinct brand personalities with memorable campaign lines, from the earliest days of Guinness – when the rules were, frankly, quite lax, and you could promise 'Guinness is good for you' – to Heineken's famously witty 'Refreshes the parts other beers cannot reach', to the inventive, original Stella Artois campaign, 'Reassuringly expensive'. Italian-brewed Peroni Nastro Azzurro is another example of a highly distinctive brand personality. It centres on elements of Italian style, with Peroni as a natural accompaniment to the good life.

From its launch in London's fashionable Sloane Street, within a boutique setting, rubbing shoulders with designer fashion houses like Emporio Armani, Emporio Peroni established its style credentials early on. They continue to interpret their concept of Italian style in a variety of fresh creative ways, achieved through their UK agency, The Bank, which specializes in a 360° approach to marketing and advertising. (We will explore this campaign further in Chapter 11, on media.) Peroni's wide-ranging approach includes their current cinema advertising, which takes off from the classic 1960s Fellini film *La Dolce Vita*.

Peroni's magazine advertising sports the now-familiar quick-reply (QR) code. In one ad, the code takes you to a trailer for a current film, and in another, to a video about Peroni's unique design initiative, Peroni Collaborazioni. This involves young designers and artists working together, and you can view their work in progress online at http://www.tumblr.com/tagged/best-of-peroni

MANDATORY ELEMENTS CONSIDERATIONS FOR THE FIGURE 8 BRIEF

In the food category, there will be certain legal requirements if the product claims to address a medical problem, for example, to reduce cholesterol. Research figures to support this claim would be mandatory. Figure 8 is not making any such claims, so any mandatory requirements would come from the client, including, for example, the name of the product, the logo.

We established in the last two chapters that the protein contained in Figure 8 is its main support, or attribute, even though it isn't a competitive factor in Mark's choice of yoghurt. Protein is important because it gives Mark the sustained energy he needs. So client and agency agree to make protein a mandatory element. A simple phrase such as this makes sense: 'contains 5g of protein per 120g pot'. This gives you the creative freedom to include that information in whatever way suits the executions. And when you talk to Mark about sustained energy, the support will always be there.

What about the flavours? Are they mandatory elements? Let's suppose Figure 8 comes in eight flavours that have proved popular with men in other foods: raspberry, strawberry, cherry, banana, blueberry, vanilla, ginger and apricot. If agency and client agree to making these mandatory, you have to include them. You could argue that at least two should be featured in every execution. All eight might clutter the ads.

Briefs are meant to steer the creative work into the best possible campaign. If there is a disagreement, a lively discussion is worth having – ideally before the brief is signed off. What if the client is very keen on seeing the whole range of flavours in each execution? One way around this common problem might be to reach an agreement that all eight flavours will be mentioned in each ad, but that a minimum of one (or two) will be shown.

Another way of handling the issue is to agree to whatever the client wants. (In the words of a leading advertising creative who shall remain nameless: 'If the client wants a big logo, / want a big logo.') Then do the best creative work you can and see how it turns out. You will have to show alternative solutions, with and without all eight flavours. Who knows? Maybe showing all eight gives you great ideas for each execution. But if including all the flavours clutters up each ad, be prepared to stand your ground. All you can do is put forward a reasoned argument and the best work you can create. With any luck, the client might agree with your recommendation.

Write on your brief:
Mandatory elements – all eight flavours must be mentioned in each ad, but only one has to be shown in each execution.

1. PRODUCT/SERVICE
2. OBJECTIVE
3. TARGET MARKET
4. STRATEGY
5. PROPOSITION
6. SUPPORT
7. COMPETITION
8. MANDATORY ELEMENTS

9. TONE OF VOICE
DESCRIBE THE CAMPAIGN'S CHARACTER – IN THREE ADJECTIVES, MAX!

10. DESIRED CONSUMER RESPONSE
11. MEDIA REQUIREMENT

This section of the brief defines the campaign's character in just a few words, giving you valuable clues as to what the look, feel and sound of your creative solutions should be. Keeping to a maximum of three descriptive words forces the agency and client to pinpoint a precise tone of voice. When you are given a brief, that precision enables you to create a campaign with the agreed tone of voice. If you are creating a new campaign for an existing client, working on a new business pitch, or on your portfolio, *you* will determine how to achieve that tone of voice from the start. It's an exciting challenge.

'Tone of voice' stems from word-based literature and media. But in advertising, the term refers to the overall character derived from both visual and verbal elements, across whatever media you're using. Tone of voice includes not only the spoken words on TV, radio and cinema ads, but also imagery, music and sound effects. In digital and print-based media, your decisions on design, layout, typography, colour, in addition to the copy, all contribute to your campaign's overall tone of voice. And if you use a celebrity, visually, or as a voiceover, your campaign's tone of voice, especially if it is well established, steers the choice of celebrity. You will need to decide which celebrity's personality best complements your campaign's personality.

Memorable campaigns have a clearly defined tone of voice. As a consumer, you might never consciously define it, but when it is coherent and consistent, you feel you 'know' the brand even before you see the logo at the end of a commercial, or in the corner of a poster. It is one of the key unifying elements of any campaign, and in some cases continues for years to project this well-defined character to its audience.

The irreverent, sensible, understated tone of voice of VW is vividly executed in this brilliant 1969 commercial. When we learn that 'sensible' Harold, owner of a 'sensible' VW, is to inherit a fortune by virtue of driving that 'sensible' car, it raises a smile.

You can be tempted by many factors to go 'off key'. Maybe a certain celebrity isn't available, or a piece of music is too expensive, or the global reach of the business

means that certain decisions are forced onto every agency, some of which result in solutions that don't mesh with the established tone of voice. Another temptation is to imitate a current, popular campaign approach, or to base your executions on an amazing new visual treatment from a blockbuster movie. Clients and agencies are prone to these temptations. Resist! All of these situations can compromise a consistent tone of voice, one that is unique and suits the brand you're working on.

WHAT DETERMINES THE TONE OF VOICE?

The tone of voice is not something a planner plucks out of thin air, hoping for the best. It is determined by two elements: your audience and your objective. Think about how, in normal conversation, you change your tone of voice, sometimes only slightly, sometimes a great deal, depending on the same two things: the person you are talking to (audience) and what you are trying to achieve (objective). This still leaves room for choice in terms of deciding on the most effective tone of voice to advertise a particular product or service. What else comes into the mix?

The nature of the product or service itself. Client and agency have to agree on the essential character of what is being advertised to determine the tone of voice. Of course, these decisions are not always made in the neat and tidy stages that the creative brief document represents. Especially in a new business pitch, the agency often needs to leap ahead and present creative work in a tone of voice that is totally unexpected by the client. If the creative work meets the objective and the agency can convince the client that it will attract the audience, the client will agree that, however surprising, the tone of voice is appropriate and highly effective for the brand – unifying the creative work for years to come. An example of this sequence of events is DDB's long-running, successful advertising for VW which, amazingly, has maintained a consistent, unique tone of voice across different markets for decades.

TONE OF VOICE AND STIMULUS

Irreverent. Sensible. Understated. These words characterize VW's tone of voice from the first ads, which Bill Bernbach created at DDB NY in the 1960s, to the latest global campaigns. 'Funny' is not among the three words. Yet VW campaigns have always raised a smile. 'Funny' is not a tone of voice. It is an audience response. Your audience decides what is funny – you can only create the stimulus to make that happen. Comedy writers know that one of the best ways to do this is within a serious scenario. The early VW commercial, 'Funeral' (shown on the previous page), is a classic example. The voiceover is a man reading his will, as if from beyond the grave, detailing why his flashy relatives will receive 'Nothing! Nothing! Nothing!', while his sensible nephew, who drives a VW, will inherit everything. The wry humour comes from watching the relatives' unseemly riotous behaviour, unaware they have been disinherited. The objective is met, and we cannot help but side with Harold, the tearful nephew.

However unfair the grounds for comparison, an overall tone of voice, including how a politician looks and sounds, can be more important than the content of their message, and it is how a majority of people make their judgements. The young, open-looking Kennedy won the debate, and the election, over the older Nixon with his furrowed brow.

In the late 1980s, Bernbach's colleague Bob Levenson, chairman of DDB International and worldwide creative director commented: 'In the end, the manufacturing philosophy and the advertising philosophy became one and the same. Volkswagen spoke with one voice throughout the world, and people everywhere recognized that voice.'

UNDERSTANDING THE EXISTING TONE OF VOICE

When you receive a brief for a campaign that is up and running, the tone of voice will be established. Part of your job as a creative is to understand what that tone of voice is so that you don't feel trapped by it. You want to be able to create executions that reflect that tone of voice, but in fresh ways. The best way to understand the brand's tone of voice is to look at the advertising. Consider the 2011 VW press ad we looked at in Chapter Five (p.115), the utter simplicity of the visual, the cleverness of making you move your head from side to side, with the copy – 'no need to shake your head' – catching you out as you do it, adds up to a tone of voice that, more than 50 years after it was established, is recognizably that of VW.

THE IMPORTANCE OF TONE OF VOICE

If you ignore the importance of the tone of voice, you could unwittingly create a campaign that alienates your target audience. No matter how clear the objective, and how deep the strategic insight, if you speak to someone in the wrong tone of voice, the campaign will not work.

Many politicians learn this to their cost. It isn't just what they say, or even how they speak, that affects our view of them. It is also how they look, their stance, what their body language says to us. Whether this is a good or a bad thing is the subject of lively debate. However, the facts remain that an audience reacts consciously and unconsciously to visual and verbal cues as much as it does to the content of a politician's speech. You can learn a great deal from observing the political scene and the audience's reaction to various leaders.

For example, in most countries, a measured, calm, yet authoritative tone is more likely to convince an audience than a hectoring rant. If the politician has a worried, 'shifty' look, the audience will tend not to trust that person, and will respond in a negative way. TV proved to be the downfall of Richard Nixon in the famous televised debates in 1960 with John F. Kennedy, whose youthful good looks and open and appealing manner contrasted sharply with Nixon's furrowed brow, five o'clock shadow and unfortunate tendency to sweat under the hot TV lights. Interestingly, those who followed the debate on the radio thought Nixon had won.

DISTINCTIVE TONES OF VOICE

A good agency is distinguished by its ability to give each of its clients a distinctive tone of voice. If all their clients 'sound the same', or 'look the same', it is the agency's tone of voice that predominates, rather than that of the individual brands. Clients notice this, and it is not good news for any agency when they do. Achieving a distinctive tone of voice for each client throughout your portfolio is equally important. It shows you have a range of visual and verbal skills to solve each client's problem with a different tone of voice, one which suits that product or service.

Adjectives that could describe the tone of voice of this campaign include arresting, stylish, transgressive, daring, erotic. Add your own, then decide: which *three* would you choose?

1   2

BUILD UP YOUR VOCABULARY

An ongoing exercise to help you make each campaign distinctive is to observe the various tones of voice that characterize successful campaigns, current and classic. Try to pin down in a few words their tone of voice. Campaigns that lack personality, whose objective is fuzzy, are harder to describe in a precise way. They are bland and less memorable. Choose a few of those campaigns too, to see the difference. Before long you will build up a vocabulary of descriptive adjectives which will help you define your own creative approach, as well as the competitor's. We have just explored VW's tone of voice. Let's continue with a few more examples from earlier chapters and define their tone of voice. The Italian campaign for Stella's coffee maker (opposite) is memorable. The ads fulfil the objective: to convey the intensity, or 'bite', of strong coffee, which the target market loves. To define its tone of voice, consider every aspect of the ad, visual and verbal. Keep in mind its objective and the audience. Make a list of descriptive adjectives and pare it down to three key words.

1   Make the most of your tone of voice by using it consistently throughout your communication. Innocent has a fresh, honest and informative tone that is established through its brand name and use of clean graphics, and extends throughout its verbal and visual communication.

2   Creating the tone of voice for a new product gives you the opportunity to create a new language. Use that language to make the brand distinctive, as Innocent has done, from the product's name to every other aspect of communication, including the packaging.

MAKE THE BEST USE OF YOUR TONE OF VOICE

How would you describe the tone of voice of the Innocent brand, which we looked at in Chapter One? Fresh, honest and informative are certainly three key defining words. You might choose other, similar words. If you consider these three words – fresh, honest, informative – they may not be unique to Innocent. However, Innocent is unique in making the best use of this tone of voice – understanding it, extending it to all its communication and remaining true to it.

The tone of voice began with the name 'Innocent' and the halo graphic. The team used the packaging to talk to the consumer in fresh, engaging ways about their ingredients. And the advertising kept to the same tone. The brand, which now extends to orange juice, speaks with a single voice in every medium, and this strengthens its impact. It seems a simple thing, but look at the orange juice label copy: 'never ever from concentrate'. The additional word, 'ever', appears unnecessary. But it is a creative touch that reflects Innocent's consistent, memorable tone of voice.

VARIATIONS WITHIN AN OVERALL TONE OF VOICE

Highly competitive markets demand that you create a tone of voice that distinguishes your brand visually and verbally. Your advertising needs to set itself apart, yet stay on strategy. For example, in the bottled-water category, the tone of voice of several brands is 'pristine, natural, elemental'. Brand-leader Evian, with its Alpine heritage well established, has met the challenge of creating a distinctive tone of voice exemplified by two successful campaigns, 'Roller Babies', and 'T-shirt'. These approaches differ creatively, as we saw when we explored Evian's strategic approach in Chapter Four. When the expression of Evian's strategy, 'live young', moved on from babies doing stunts to a vibrant series of individuals reacting to one another, the point of view shifted, and, with it, the tone. In the 'T-shirt' campaign, as Michael Aidan, Evian's global brand director, noted, 'the baby is in you'.

Both campaigns are energetic, quirky, full of life. You could sum up the tone of voice for both with those words. You could be more concise and use one French expression, *joie de vivre*, 'the joy of living'. However, 'T-shirt' is people-centred. To put it another way, with 'Roller Babies' you are the observer watching the babies' amazing antics, while with 'T-shirt' you are likely to feel more part of the action. To define this shift in tone, you could add a word like 'sociable' to *joie de vivre*.

MUSIC HELPS TO DEFINE THE TONE OF VOICE

Music is a powerful creative element in TV, cinema, online, mobile phone and radio advertising. Even a few notes can define a brand. For years, Castrol Oil's

1

2   3

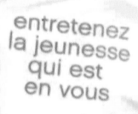

1   This still from Evian's commercial 'Roller Babies' expresses a tone of voice that could be described as energetic, quirky, full of life. Or simply, *joie de vivre*.

2   In 'T-shirt', the Evian campaign that followed 'Roller Babies', the introduction of people communicating with each other and the audience shifts the point of view and the tone of voice.

3   The two Evian campaigns maintain a consistent tone of voice in a highly competitive category, while differing in one respect. The interaction of people in 'T-shirt' suggests that the word 'sociable' could be added to *joie de vivre* to define a subtle shift in tone from 'Roller Babies'.

entretenez
la jeunesse
qui est
en vous

'Liquid Engineering' campaign successfully used the opening notes of the second *Nachtmusik* movement of Mahler's Seventh Symphony as its signature theme. This commercial use of music infuriates lovers of rock as well as classical music, ruining their appreciation of the original because of its commercial association. A recent comment posted on an independent forum for BBC Radio 3 listeners sums it up: 'Bach's Cantata No. 147 has forever been besmirched for me since Lloyds Bank used it endlessly with that wretched black horse running through the fields.'

Nonetheless, creative people in advertising continue to use music to great effect, whether they commission original compositions or use much-loved tracks from every genre. Marvin Gaye's classic, 'I Heard It Through the Grapevine', was an integral part of the sultry, nostalgic tone of voice for BBH's Levi's 'Laundrette' commercial. Sometimes, a commercial makes a song famous. 'Get Down Saturday Night' by Oliver Cheatham didn't get above number 38 in the UK singles chart upon its release in 1983. In 2003, Room 5 remixed the song, retitling it 'Make Luv', and it was used in a famous Lynx Pulse deodorant commercial. When 'Make Luv' was released as a single shortly after the campaign, it reached number one and stayed there for four weeks.

More recently, Cadbury Dairy Milk chocolate took a man and a gorilla suit, put them together with the great Phil Collins song 'In the Air Tonight', and made the TV commercial 'Gorilla Drum'. Its tone of voice is warm, tongue-in-cheek and wildly satisfying. This extraordinary commercial shows how music can help to define the tone of voice, and create an emotional response that words alone could never achieve. It is the choice of this evocative music against the visual of the gorilla that creates a distinctive tone of voice. All the elements in a commercial play a part.

The surprising image of the gorilla alerts us that something 'is in the air tonight': something unusual is about to happen – but what? The measured pace of the film creates a sense of anticipation – the gorilla's face expresses a longing for something to happen. Suddenly, everything comes alive. The juxtaposition of the incredibly romantic lyrics, 'I've been waiting for this moment all my life', with the sad-eyed gorilla bursting into joyous drumming is a brilliant piece of film-making.

The gorilla's transformation, from sad to satisfied, is triggered by the song's lyrics. This moment makes you smile however many times you watch – and hear – it. The commercial's warm-hearted, tongue-in-cheek, wildly satisfying tone of voice is distinctive within the confectionery category, amidst advertising that is often overly sentimental and predictable. The tone of voice introduces the joy of eating Cadbury's chocolate, as shown in the final frame, 'A glass and a half full of joy', a play on Cadbury's long-established campaign line, 'A glass and a half full of milk'.

DEFINING THE TONE OF VOICE FOR FIGURE 8

We have to decide on a tone of voice that appeals to men yet doesn't alienate women, Figure 8's current audience. It is always a risk to extend a brand's appeal to a new target market, because you might lose some of the market you have, and not get the new one. It's important to set the right tone of voice. Tone of voice depends on three things: the person you are talking to, your objective, and the nature of the product itself. Let's review these elements.

1.   Mark likes yoghurt. He is confident enough to take advice from his girlfriend/wife, and we have said that once he finds something he likes – even if it's not aimed at him – he would choose it, given the right advertising message. You might have written some additional details to help you get a clear picture of Mark and his life.

2.   Our objective is to encourage Mark not to resist buying Figure 8 for himself.

3.   We know that Figure 8 would provide Mark with an excellent source of protein which would keep up his energy until lunch.

One way to help you determine an appropriate tone of voice is to look at what other brands sound and look like. You want Mark to notice your advertising. Most brands have a tone of voice that includes the word 'healthy'. Can you say this in a way that

defines the personality of your advertising more precisely and distinctively? 'Energetic' is a good word to set the tone for a healthy yoghurt. 'Energetic' will help you think about imagery and pace when you're working on your creative ideas, while still conveying the healthy aspect of the product.

Mark likes to think of himself as the kind of guy who relishes a challenge. He has a mind of his own, and really doesn't care what people think. As your second word to describe the tone of voice, 'challenging' would give you the freedom to explore various executional directions.

Finally, something to do with taste appeal would suit this approach, since Mark is having Figure 8 on days when he is on his own. The word 'irresistible' or 'tempting' could be the third word. Maybe you can think of better adjectives than these. For now, if you put these three words in this section it will give you a good start: energetic, challenging, irresistible.

10. DESIRED CONSUMER RESPONSE

WHAT DO YOU WANT YOUR TARGET AUDIENCE TO DO,
FEEL OR THINK AFTER SEEING THE ADVERTISING?

This section of the brief describes how you would like your audience to respond to your advertising. Defining the response as precisely as you can sets a benchmark for what you and the client hope to achieve from your creative work. Whether you are determining the ideal response to one ad, or to an entire campaign, it has to be realistic.

'Response' is the final element in what Jeremy Bullmore identifies as advertising's 'communication chain': sender, receiver, medium, stimulus and response. We explored this interplay of stimulus and response in Chapter Five from the point of view of the stimulus – the proposition. Now we're concentrating on the response.

You and your planner will have considered this question – what do you want your target audience to think, feel and do after seeing the advertising? – throughout the creative brief process. Since you won't yet have created any advertising, you have to imagine the audience's response to your proposition. This stimulus, together with your knowledge of the target market, helps you define the response you want.

Of course, you can never fully predict or control a person's reaction to your communication. Different factors influence people's response: the impact of the creative executions, the competition, choice of media, and external factors such as the state of the economy. However, you still need a plan. And your strategic thinking skills, combined with your imaginative ability to put yourself in someone else's shoes, will help you define a realistic ideal response to your advertising.

THINK, FEEL OR DO

To 'do' something obviously implies an action. This can be an end in itself – to try something new, for example. It could also lead to a further action that meets your objective. For example, if a consumer responds to a car ad by taking a test drive, this could ultimately lead to them buying that car. To 'feel' a certain way involves an emotional response. This can lead to action – such as giving to a charity. To 'think' in a new way requires a mental shift. This shift might happen quickly, or over time, before it leads to action: to give up smoking, for example; to vote for a different political party; or, as we'll see, to switch your brand of computer.

This section of the brief defines for you and the client, a realistic ideal response to your advertising (as shown in this artwork by Terry Hamaton illustrating the final link in Jeremy Bullmore's 'chain of communication'). Putting it into words helps steer your creative work.

Although a person's response can be complex, with a mix of reactions, try to isolate the initial, key reaction you want from your advertising. That's usually the most realistic response you can achieve. There is no 'best' response. Nor does the product's category determine the 'right' response. Each brief is unique, with its own specific approach to a problem. The desired consumer response should reflect this.

THINK

You cannot achieve everything at once in a campaign. And if you skip a stage in addressing your target audience, you might not achieve what you want from your overall campaign. So, for example, it might be that your initial campaign needs first of all to shift your target audience's opinion within a category – not to act differently, or at least not yet. Perhaps you are looking for the audience to undergo a mental shift: to think differently. Chiat/Day's 1997 US campaign for Apple famously crystallized this desired consumer response in the campaign line, 'Think different'.

With its iconic photographs of great artists and innovators, the campaign reinvigorated Apple's image as a visionary, inventive company whose new marketing strategy, under Steve Jobs, was being streamlined in an effort to return it to its former glory. Even the campaign line's grammar was 'different', in that an adjective was being used as an adverb: 'Think different' instead of 'Think differently'. And apparently Apple got some flak for that. But, as a creative, you have the freedom and the licence to play with words and grammar to make the most impact possible. 'Think different' works brilliantly. (Or is that 'brilliant'?)

Consumer response was immediate and positive to this decidedly non-technological, conceptual campaign. Lee Clow, Chiat/Day's creative director, who wrote the campaign line 'Think different', worked closely with Apple to oversee what turned out to be an award-winning advertising approach which ran until 2002.

This example, with Albert Einstein's inimitable shock of hair and pensive expression, is one of many posters that ran during Apple's campaign, featuring thinkers, celebrities and artists, from Pablo Picasso to Bob Dylan. Complementary posters were sent to schools across America, as the ads went up on major outdoor billboard sites. Apple was the first computer company to use fashion and general interest (non-computer) magazines, as well as billboards, to shift opinion, and regain their previous counter-cultural image, which they had largely lost in the past decade. This campaign achieved their initial desired consumer response: to think differently about Apple. To consider the brand as inspiring and visionary with inventive, imaginative ideas – not just another computer company. Product sales followed.

1

1　　The initial desired consumer response to this Apple campaign was to think differently, rather than rush out and buy an Apple computer. No computer products were shown throughout this campaign.

2　　'Here's to the crazy ones' is the memorable beginning to the copy of Apple's 1997 campaign. Chiat/Day copywriter Craig Tanimoto wrote the words that formed the basis for all the TV, magazine and billboard executions.

To the crazy ones.

Here's to the crazy ones.
　　The misfits.
　　　　The rebels.
　　　　　　The troublemakers.
　　　　　　　　The round pegs in the square holes.
The ones who see things differently.

They're not fond of rules.
　　And they have no respect for the status quo.

You can praise them, disagree with them, quote them,
　　disbelieve them, glorify them or vilify them.
About the only thing you can't do is ignore them.

Because they change things.
　　They invent.　　They imagine.　　They heal.
　　They explore.　　They create.　　They inspire.
They push the human race forward.

Maybe they have to be crazy.
How else can you stare at an empty canvas and see a work of art?
　　Or sit in silence and hear a song that's never been written?
Or gaze at a red planet and see a laboratory on wheels?

We make tools for these kinds of people.
While some see them as the crazy ones, we see genius.

Because the people who are crazy enough to think they can
change the world, are the ones who do.

Think different.

2

NO DEJES QUE LA
COMIDA QUE TE GUSTA
TE HAGA DAÑO

OPPOSITE Actor Steven Berkoff
fights off an imaginary attacker
in these stills from a TV advert
about how to recognize the
onset of a heart attack. Created
by Grey London for the British
Heart Foundation, the film's
strong emotional effect remained
with viewers, an estimated 70 of
whom rang the emergency
services and saved a life because
of their greater understanding of
the symptoms.

LEFT This advertising approach
endears Pepto-Bismol to its
audience for its sympathetic, witty
approach. The stimulus creates
an emotional response, which
continues to build brand loyalty.

FEEL

You might decide that the key desired response to your campaign is an emotional one. That can be extremely powerful across many different categories, from public-service advertising, to charities and political campaigns, as well as everyday products. The above still is from 'Empanada', the US Spanish-language TV commercial for Pepto-Bismol, which we looked at in Chapter One. Its emotional selling point (ESP) engages the viewer, especially because he or she needs this product when they are feeling unwell. Pepto-Bismol is a practical, effective product – a leading, trusted remedy for adult heartburn, indigestion, upset stomach and diarrhoea. Yet the key consumer response to the campaign line – 'Don't let the food you love hurt you' – is overwhelmingly emotional: 'Pepto-Bismol is really looking after me.'

EMOTIONAL RESPONSE LEADS TO ACTION

An emotional response can lead surprisingly quickly to a person taking action, from donating money from their mobile during a charity telethon, to making a life-saving phone call following a campaign about the symptoms of a heart attack.

On 10 August 2008, six million viewers of the UK commercial TV channel ITV1 watched a two-minute film showing a simulated series of symptoms of a heart attack (opposite). There were posters, print and radio promoting this two-minute spot, which aired only once. According to research commissioned by the British Heart Foundation, four out of five viewers had a better understanding of these symptoms following this commercial. They estimate that 70 people survived heart attacks that would have killed them had they or someone with them not called for an ambulance so quickly as a result of seeing the film.

Ultimately, the goal of most advertising campaigns is to persuade people to buy

something, donate money, vote for a particular candidate – in other words, to 'do' something. However, as you've seen throughout the creative-brief process, asking someone outright to 'do' whatever it is you want, does not always achieve the desired effect. Your campaign's proposition provides a stimulus for an initial consumer response, which should lead, ultimately, to your goal. It has to be supported by valid reasons, communicated in an appropriate tone of voice.

For example, the desired audience response might be to feel that donating to a charity is worthwhile. This leaves it to the audience to close the circle, and decide on their own terms to take action, which, in this example, means giving money. By never asking overtly for money, people might give more than they otherwise would. The Spanish commercial 'Team Hoyt', which we looked at in Chapter Two, had as its objective: 'to convince viewers about the importance of their donations in fighting against spinal cord and brain injuries'. The TV commercial shows the extraordinary father-and-son team of Rick and his father Dick Hoyt. Together, the pair have participated in over 900 endurance tests and six 'Ironman' triathlons. Their achievements inspired the viewing audience. The final frame shows a telephone number to respond to, but no mention was made of contributions.

EMOTION AND TRUST

You might expect that action – 'to do' something – would be the desired response to a practical range of products. Yet, surprising as it may seem, an emotional response – belief in product performance – can prove an incredibly successful way forward. Trusting product performance is an emotional consumer response, difficult to achieve, and one which hundreds of clients and their agencies would desire from their advertising, across every category.

A clear example of a brand that achieves this response from its advertising is Ronseal. We touched on the campaign in Chapter Five. The overall campaign line is: 'Ronseal. It does exactly what it says on the tin.' This phrase has entered the language in the UK, and become synonymous with trusting a product, a brand, and even a person. The popularity of this phrase comes from the lack of performance of so many products and services – they overpromise, and people feel let down. In the DIY category, underperforming products lead to frustration, a

1

2

3   4

1   Male voiceover: 'This is Ronseal Quick-Drying Woodstain.'

2   'You can't miss it. It comes in a tin, with Ronseal Quick-Drying Woodstain on it.'

3   'It protects and it's rainproof in about 30 minutes. Which means, in about 30 minutes, your wood's rainproof and protected.'

4   'So if you've got wood to stain and you want it to dry quickly, use Ronseal Quick-Drying Woodstain. It does exactly what it says on the tin.'

1   2

loss of confidence in a brand, as well as a loss of self-confidence, especially if a person is attempting a project which is a bit challenging to begin with.

Ronseal's advertising approach has been to state in a consciously straightforward way this all-too-often unfulfilled consumer desire for a product to perform as it says it will. This long-running campaign, launched in 1994 by London agency HHCL, continues to this day. The now-famous campaign line was created by Liz Whiston and Dave Shelton. The word 'tin' is used to cover all their products, no matter what they come in. The no-frills tone of voice of Ronseal's advertising – the presenter's face, his down-to-earth delivery – the pared-down visuals and simple, repetitious copy, are all contributing factors in eliciting an emotional response from the viewer. The desired consumer response – 'I feel confident this product will work' – has led to a brand-building campaign. Needless to say, when you run strong advertising like this, the products have to perform.

1   In this engaging 2002 Italian commercial for Fiat, created by Leo Burnett Milan, the older player seizes the moment. He pops a chess piece into his mouth, ruining the younger player's chance to 'checkmate' him.

2   This commercial, which offers zero per cent interest financing for a limited time, reveals the deadline at the end of the ad. The desired consumer response is to act quickly, or 'seize the moment'.

DO

If you want the initial response of your target audience to involve action – consumers doing something in response to your advertising – you need to convey a sense of urgency. For example, advertising a special promotion within a limited time period means your desired consumer reaction will be action-oriented to take advantage of the offer. How you achieve this, creatively, is up to you. It doesn't have to be a fast-paced execution with a frantic soundtrack. It could be just the opposite.

In Chapter Two, we looked at the witty Italian Fiat commercial, 'Chess Game', in which the objective was to offer customers zero per cent financing with a deadline. The commercial unfolds at the slow pace of a typical chess game. The younger player, momentarily distracted by a phone ringing, turns away. His older opponent seizes the opportunity to win the game by a sleight of hand – popping a large chess piece into his mouth. That one action stands out, evoking the desired audience response to 'seize the moment' – to grab the finance deal that Fiat is offering.

ACTION AND POLITICS

Political advertising ultimately requires an active response from the target audience. *Thinking* about voting, or feeling that you *should* vote, are both important responses and can prepare the ground for a person actually going to the polls and casting a ballot. But at a critical stage in the run-up to an election, the response you want and need from your target audience is action – as many people as possible turning up on the day to vote for the candidate your advertising supports.

One of the most lateral and brilliant political campaigns designed to achieve this active, positive response was 'The Great Schlep', a viral commercial created by Droga5, an American agency led by the charismatic Australian David Droga.

The campaign's objective was to get the 'swing' state of Florida to vote Democratic and help elect Barack Obama in 2008. A 'swing' state is one whose votes can be decisive in the final tally, with the potential to win or lose the overall presidential election for a political party. In 2000, Florida had swung Republican, giving George W. Bush the presidency instead of his Democratic opponent, Al Gore.

Florida has a large Jewish population, but would they bother to vote, and would they vote for Obama? Instead of targeting them directly, Droga5 used a different strategy. By encouraging younger people from other states who were confirmed Obama supporters to go and visit their Jewish relatives in Florida and convince them to vote for Obama, the state would swing Democratic. Obama would win.

The audience responded. They made the great 'schlep' – originally a Yiddish term meaning 'journey' – thanks to a terrific performance by US comedian Sarah Silverman. This viral, over four minutes long, is well worth your time to look at in full online. It's highly entertaining, serious, frank – and full of humanity.

Silverman's plea to the audience provided good reasons to make the 'schlep' and suggested ways to convince a Jewish relative living in Florida why he or she should vote Democratic. Whatever your politics, this viral campaign achieved its desired audience response.

Selected frames, to give you the flavour of the commercial, follow.

1	2
3	4
5	6
7	8

1   Sarah Silverman: 'If you knew that visiting your grandparents would change the world, would you do it? Of course you would. You'd have to be a douche-nozzle not to.'

2   'Hey, it's Sarah. ... Silverman.'

3   'If Barack Obama doesn't become the next president of the United States, I'm going to blame the Jews.'

4   'Jews are the most scrappy, liberal, civil rights people there are – yes – that's true. But you're forgetting a whole large group of Jews that are not that way, and they go by several aliases.'

5   'Nana, Papa, Zadie, Boobie, plain old grandma and grandpa ...'

6   'These are the people who vote in Florida. The Florida vote can make or break an election.'

7   'I'm making this video to urge you to schlep over to Florida and convince your grandparents to vote Obama. It can make the difference.'

8   End title: The Great Schlep.

THE <u>DESIRED CONSUMER RESPONSE</u> TO YOUR FIGURE 8 CAMPAIGN

To define the response you ideally want from your advertising, look at the proposition, which we arrived at in Chapter Five: 'Wake up to what your body wants, every morning. Figure 8.'

The proposition can become your campaign line – it is the stimulus to which Mark will respond. Since you haven't yet created the advertising, you can't be sure how you are going to execute the campaign, but two things seem to stand out. The proposition implies a sense of immediacy. 'Wake up' is telling Mark to pay attention – do what his body wants him to do. Also, it suggests to Mark that having Figure 8 every morning could become a welcome habit – something he won't have to think about once he makes it part of his daily ritual, whether he's with his girlfriend/wife or on his own.

These two aspects of the proposition – immediacy and habit – suggest that the response you should be looking for is action-oriented.

Buying Figure 8 for himself shouldn't become a big decision that he has to think about for weeks. Nor is it necessarily an emotional decision – although food products are often tied into emotional states of mind. Chocolate advertising, for example, evokes an emotional response which leads to a person choosing that brand, as in the Cadbury's 'Gorilla Drum'

commercial. Feeling good is the emotional response to that ad.

But yoghurt is different from chocolate. And in this particular brief, action rather than emotion seems appropriate. Although Mark should feel good after seeing your advertising, the key response you ideally want would be for him to pick up Figure 8 the next time he's in the dairy section of his supermarket. He's in there anyway, grabbing a pint of milk for his morning coffee. He should just do it – as Nike would say. What's stopping him? Ideally, it should become an irresistible habit.

Remember that we identified the tone of voice in the last chapter as 'energetic, challenging and irresistible'. Keep that in mind, and remember your proposition. 'Contains 5g of protein in every 120g pot' is your only mandatory – apart from mentioning the eight flavours and featuring one. This still gives you a lot of creative freedom.

Write on your brief:

Mark's desired response is: 'I'm going to pick up a few pots of Figure 8 tonight to see me through the week.'

11. MEDIA REQUIREMENT
WHERE WILL THE ADVERTISING APPEAR?

This final section of the creative brief examines where and when your audience will see, hear, click on, experience, and, above all, engage with your advertising across the media spectrum. You can reach your audience in so many ways: from ambient to apps, banners to branded-gaming, cinema, experiential events, magazines, posters, press, product placement in film and TV, radio, social-networking sites, sponsorship, TV, websites – and the list keeps growing. From the moment you wake up to the last thing at night, there is something new to attract your attention, potentially making it easier to shop, eat, drink, fly, drive, date, vote or donate to your favourite cause.

The choice of media determines whether your advertising will reach the right person at the right moment. What could be more important? You need to be involved in the decisions, if at all possible. Of course, you will have media professionals to help you. The increasing diversity of media, and the huge amounts of money involved, requires media specialists in two key areas: planning and buying. The media planner has a strategic role, and works alongside your agency planner to devise the most effective way of reaching your target audience. Specialist media buyers then negotiate the best deal for each medium. On small accounts, one person handles both roles. However, planning and buying a multi-channel media campaign for pan-European or global campaigns demands several people with specific skills in each area.

The cost of media varies enormously, from a free page on Facebook to a couple of hundred pounds for a banner ad, to several hundred thousand pounds for 30 seconds of TV in a peak slot. Cost is determined by the type of medium and how many people your ads reach. Other factors come into play – if a TV show, film or magazine attracts an influential and/or higher-spending consumer, that medium can command a high price. In TV, a limited number of advertising minutes per hour – as well as audience numbers – ultimately drives the price up. Or down.

TV broadcast negotiations can involve costly, last-minute decisions. Slots sold close to the time of broadcast are called 'late money'. For example, at the time of writing media buyers are trying to bring down by 15 per cent the record 2010 price of £250,000 for 30 seconds of TV advertising during the final weekend of *The X Factor*, the UK's most popular show. It's the UK equivalent of America's Super Bowl in terms of audience reach. Media buyers are arguing that because audiences for this hit talent show fell by over a million from 2010 to 2011, the price per second should reflect this. But what if audience numbers spike beyond expectation on this final December show? No advertiser wants to be left out of a potentially epic evening. It's a bit of a gamble.

The Starbucks app gives you the option to set up a pre-pay account, plus find the closest store, explore the world of coffee beans, find information about nutrition, and share your location and favourite drinks through Facebook or Twitter. It's an app, of course, as mobile as you. Many apps are a cross between a marketing tool and an advertising medium.

PUSH THE BOUNDARIES

Whatever size and type of agency you're working in, get to know the media people. They could be part of a separate company, in a different building. It is well worth making the effort. Exchanging ideas leads to more creative solutions. And

if you show an interest, media people are more likely to respond to a 'crazy' idea and help make it happen. Ideally, your creative work should influence the choice of media. But even if final decisions have been made before you see the brief, you could add to, refresh, even revolutionize the advertising approach to the media already chosen.

Boundaries change all the time and it will be up to you to break new ground with your ideas. In the Introduction, we saw how VW was the first to launch a car via digital media. Take a look at this groundbreaking Araldite poster campaign from 1983 created by Ian Potter, Rob Kitchen and Rob Janowski at FCO Univas. The apparently crazy idea turned this supersite into a traffic-stopping moment on London's busy Cromwell Road, the main artery leading out of the city to Heathrow Airport. The creative team pushed the boundaries of the product and the medium, experimenting with both.

By deciding to demonstrate the power of Araldite glue with a huge physical object – a car – stuck on a poster, the creative team from FCO Univas shifted the genre of demonstration from its traditional home, TV, to a static, normally two-dimensional medium. This one campaign changed the nature of the poster medium.

The initial poster for Araldite glue, art-directed by Ian Potter and written by Rob Kitchen, won the D&AD (Design and Art Direction) Black Pencil award, the only recipient in 1983 of this high accolade. The poster appeared first in London for a month, and was then moved to a series of six cities across the UK.

The campaign consisted of four posters. The first one was such a success that the following year the team got the idea for a sequence of three more, to tell the story over several weeks. Again, a sequential approach was more often associated with TV advertising, rather than the poster medium. Yet here was an entertaining narrative, with an added element of suspense. Rob Kitchen's understated copy for the initial poster is inspired.

Juxtaposed against the surprising evidence of a full-size car stuck on a poster, is a line of copy telling you about repairing your teapot! While you're wondering, 'Will the car fall off, and if so, when?', the copy calmly tells you in six words why you really need Araldite: 'It also sticks handles to teapots.' It's for those pesky, ordinary household tasks many glues fail to achieve. The 'also' makes you smile. The tongue-in-cheek tone gave this campaign its many admirers.

1   Pushing the boundaries of a medium changes it forever.

2   The series of four executions transfixed drivers as well as pedestrians, practically gluing passers-by to the spot. It made this brand famous.

3   The Araldite poster campaign demonstrated the product and also told a story with its sequential and increasingly astonishing feats of stickiness. This supersite turned an everyday product into a superstar. It was a media breakthrough in a prime location.

4   This was the perfect finish to the Araldite campaign. (The answer is creativity.)

Of course, thanks to the digital revolution, posters are no longer static. They light up, show films, act more like TV than posters. The only constant in the world of media is change, and your creative ideas, as well as technological advances, will bring it about.

1
2
3

We live in
FINANCIAL TIMES

1   This compelling image of the shark-infested waters of the business world, represents large companies swallowing smaller ones in the mergers-and-acquisitions process. It attracts new, and younger, global business people, who need analysis and in-depth coverage, to the *FT*.

2   The global economy is represented by clustering famous skyscrapers from the world's key business centres on one island. The *FT* is online, and is read globally. This emphasizes to a wider audience the need to read the *FT*, in whichever form, wherever you do business.

3   The face of Richard Branson, superimposed on the iconic photo of the South American revolutionary Che Guevara, draws a highly ambitious and younger global audience to the *FT*. They're hungry for insight into entrepreneurs who turn companies around, or start them from scratch. The initial media buy for the new *FT* poster campaign included key commuter sites in London and south-east England, where the advertising began. It expanded globally later that year and continues to run with equally fresh and inventive executions. The web address on the posters leads viewers to the *FT's* interactive website. The DDB team responsible for the campaign was creative director Adam Tucker, and creative teams Victor Monclus and Will Lowe, Matt Lee and Pete Heyes, Damien Bellon and Thierry Albert, and head of art Grant Parker.

THE CONTINUING POWER OF THE POSTER

The poster has always been an ideal medium for expressing a campaign's essence, its proposition, in a compelling way. In the highly fragmented media scene, with so many channels of communication, the poster has experienced a resurgence in popularity as a means of unifying a campaign. Posters are often accompanied by some form of digital media. Unlike ads on TV and the internet, you can't fast-forward, delete, or block a poster site. The global advertising campaign for the *Financial Times* created in 2007 by DDB London is a powerful example of the poster medium working in combination with online advertising. The media extended to branded taxis, point of sale and direct marketing. The *FT* launched its campaign in response to research findings conducted worldwide, which revealed that non-readers, and especially younger managers, perceived the *FT* as a highly respected and intelligent paper, but a bit old-fashioned and inaccessible. 'We live in Financial Times', the brilliant campaign line, speaks to a wider audience without compromising existing, core readers. Not easy to do.

This campaign seeks to reach everyone whose profession relies on understanding the tension-filled state of the world economy, not only senior management or those working directly with financial products. These arresting, imaginative images engage a younger global audience. Each poster highlights a pertinent topic explored in the *FT*: mergers and acquisitions, world business, and business revolutionaries.

THE CHALLENGE OF REACHING YOUR AUDIENCE

Just as there is no 'right' tone of voice for a particular category, there is no 'right' medium to reach your particular audience. The media choice depends on your creative ideas, who you need to reach, and when. And the size of the budget.

The *FT*'s global 'We Live in Financial Times' campaign used a series of posters leading viewers to an interactive website, branded taxis, direct mail, and banner advertising on the newspaper's online edition. Honda's pan-European 'The Power of Dreams' campaign, which we will look at later, consisted of a mix of TV advertising linked to a branded mobile game, press and magazine ads, and sponsorship. Two campaigns with two completely different media combinations.

THE AGE OF THE APP

The UK supermarket Sainsbury's went for a long-running TV campaign led by a famous personality, supported by magazines, posters, online presence and an app, all designed to encourage the audience to engage fully with the brand. The 'Try Something New Today' campaign featured celebrity chef Jamie Oliver. His highly

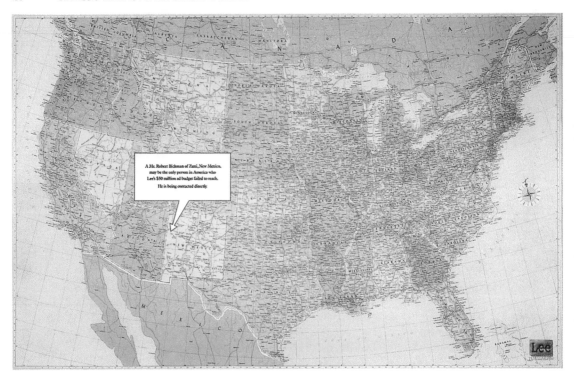

successful, user-friendly app, launched in 2009, marked the start of advertisers and agencies realizing the potential of this mobile medium. The app acted as an advertising medium for Jamie Oliver, as well as a source of advertising and additional revenue for Sainsbury's, where people could shop for Jamie's recipe ingredients. Again, the app is part advertising, part marketing tool. The link was perfect! What made this work? Sainsbury's customers (as well as non-customers) wanted the app for its appetizing content. Following its lead, many other clients want to develop an app, but they don't always understand why. To engage your audience, you need an app that people want to use for its own sake.

Ajaz Ahmed, founder of agency AKQA, which advised Volkswagen on the launch of its new-model GTI via digital media, stated in 2009 that mobiles were 'the fastest growth area in our business' (*The Guardian*, 9 November 2009). In the same interview he claimed: 'The great thing is the iPhone and App Store base has reached a critical mass.'

Ahmed has been proved right, and apps now seem to be a given for most clients, but they need to offer more than just an ad. As Jason Gurwin emphasizes in the headline for a post in his *Harvard Business Review* blog, 'Building a mobile app is not a mobile strategy' (21 November 2011). He cites the mobile analytics firm Distimo, which in 2011 claimed that 91 of the top 100 brands had their own mobile app – double the figure 18 months previously. But, as Gurwin points out, 'no one wants to download an ad'. Which is what was so clever about Jamie Oliver's original app, as well as that for the VW GTI.

Jamie Oliver's free app offered plenty of tips, as well as recipes, and then charged for additional meal ideas, thus combining free with paid-for content.

This award-winning trade ad for Lee Jeans, written by Luke Sullivan and art-directed by Arty Tan at Fallon McElligott, dramatizes the challenge of reaching your target audience, especially in a country the size of the US. Your eye goes straight to the copy, which reveals the budget.

And how big does a budget need to be to reach your audience? The cost varies enormously, even within one medium. To develop an app can cost anything from £2,000 to £50,000, and much more. Gurwin, again, notes: 'If you are a billion-dollar company, you shouldn't only be investing $50,000 in mobile. It's like airing a bad TV commercial ... it will not end in the desired result.'

Product placement can be free, if the product appears on an obscure website. Or it can cost up to $50 million, which is what Ford are said to have paid for their Aston Martin cars to appear in the James Bond films. Again, the cost is relative. And one of the misconceptions is that digital can be cheaply made yet create a huge impact. This is sometimes true, but not always.

More than half of US clients and agencies plan to increase their spend on display ads on social-media sites like Facebook over the next year, according to the eMarketer blog (26 March 2012). In comparison, only 29 per cent planned to increase their spending in magazines. There is a lot of room for growth for advertisers in social media and mobile, so it is really up to agencies to make the best use of this growth.

HOMING IN ON YOUR TARGET

How you reach people and engage with them depends on your idea and how much you have to spend. For Lee Jeans, the budget for its 1992 US advertising was $50 million. This wonderfully inventive trade ad (opposite) announces how the company met the challenge of reaching everyone in their audience with its advertising spend of $50 million. Well, *almost* everyone! Trade ads are aimed at the people who sell and distribute your clients' products, in this case Lee Jeans. If it learns about the amount of advertising support the brand will get, the trade is encouraged to stock the product. In this ad, Lee's agency, Fallon McElligott, shows a huge detailed map of the US, emphasizing the media challenge Lee faces. The witty copy makes Lee sound humble, yet triumphant. Even though Lee spent $50 million to advertise their jeans, music to the trade, there is one person whom they have yet to reach. The company plans to contact him directly. An award-winning ad, and no wonder.

'GOING VIRAL' EXTENDS YOUR REACH

There are ads that strike such a chord with the audience that within minutes they send the commercial whizzing around the net. The ad – usually a TV ad – has 'gone viral', reaching hundreds, then thousands, even millions of people, to the delight of the client and agency. That's why clients whisper a plea to their agency, 'do a viral'. Who wouldn't want to get millions of free viewings? Of course, you can never predict what will go viral. Just create the best ads you can. Only the audience will decide.

When an ad goes viral, it is great PR. That can raise the profile of a brand, but does it actually sell the product you're advertising? Logically, you would think that virals always sell the product. If you share your favourite commercial with like-minded people, you are all in the same target audience. Clearly, it isn't that simple. Your best friend might have the same sense of humour, but not the same taste in chocolate.

Cadbury's award-winning 'Gorilla Drum' commercial by Fallon, which we examined in Chapter Nine, was named the favourite TV ad of 2007. This was out of 4,000 TV ads produced that year. The website www.tellyAds.com, which runs the poll, bases its figures on the number of times each clip is viewed online. According to the website's founder, Jon Cousins, the Cadbury commercial broke all records for uploads, with over 600 postings on YouTube. These uploads accumulated about 10 million individual viewings in 2007 alone. So you won't be surprised to learn that a spokeswoman for Cadbury reported that: 'The advert has been a huge success and it has positively affected sales of this product'. The effect on sales depends on how 'big' the viral goes. 'Eyebrows', the follow-up to Cadburys' 'Gorilla' was viewed online four million times, so even a small proportion of that figure is bound to be in the right target market. Not all virals sell the product. But since you can't plan for it, just do your best.

LINKING MULTI-CHANNEL MEDIA

Most media plans include two or more different ways for the advertising to reach the right audience at the right moment. A multi-channel media plan needs to be linked by a strong concept, often expressed by the campaign line, as well as by the overall tone of voice of the executions. The aim is for your audience to respond to a seamless and engaging campaign in whichever medium they encounter it. This can only happen when an agency functions in an integrated way, enabling creative and media people to explore these different areas, yet remain focused on the brand's core concept and personality.

Wieden + Kennedy (W+K) do this especially well for Honda. They embrace several media platforms to advertise the brand, including sponsorship of TV documentaries, and features on Honda's bold initiative, the Honda Dream Factory, all within their campaign, 'The Power of Dreams'.

We saw in Chapter Five how this concept sprang from the thinking of Honda's founder, Soichiro Honda. It follows that W+K sets the pace for inventive, engaging approaches to new and traditional media, linking them conceptually and technically. It takes real collaboration to achieve these results.

W+K's spring 2011 pan-European campaign for the Honda Jazz centred on a 60-second TV commercial, accompanied by a series of print ads and an iPhone app. This app enabled viewers to 'catch' characters from the TV ad through sound, in a way that has never been achieved before.

1   The 60-second TV commercial for the Honda Jazz follows a man through his life, and this iPhone app 'catches' characters from the ad, so that the viewer can play with them. W+K creative directors Chris Groom and Sam Heath didn't want to create a microsite, or something separate from the TV ad, and this was their groundbreaking solution n.

2   You can 'grab' up to seven characters with your iPhone, while in front of your TV, using sound-synching technology linking from the soundtrack. This two-screen idea breaks new ground in interactivity. Mobile gaming is addictive. Playing with Honda's 'Jazz' characters offers a bit of fun.

The campaign, 'This Unpredictable Life', is underpinned by Honda's long-running line: 'The Power of Dreams'. Its dream-like quality contrasts with the practicality of the car itself. According to creative directors Chris Groom and Sam Heath, the everyday tasks for which this car is perfect involve unpredictable aspects. 'The Jazz is engineered to cope with these changing demands. We tried to dramatize that in the most engaging way possible.'

The campaign was featured in *Creative Review* (March 2011) with various comments, mostly praising W+K's inventiveness although some had reservations about how rewarding, and ultimately engaging, the experience was of 'grabbing' the characters and playing with them. Perhaps the most significant comment comes from Jon Williams, chief digital officer at Grey EMEA, who said: 'It's always hard doing something first. You have to do the icebreaking for those who follow, and for that I applaud those who slaved to get this to work.'

The series of three print ads amplify the theme of 'This Unpredictable Life'. Their freewheeling visuals and evocative copy express the forward-looking, inventive concept of 'The Power of Dreams'. There is a degree of unpredictability to each day, however slight, and on a bigger scale, about where the future will take us. This campaign for the Honda Jazz, a forward-looking, practical hybrid model, reflects both of these aspects.

The print campaign is unmistakably linked to the TV campaign, which, together with the iPhone app, contribute to a focused, multi-channel media approach for the Honda Jazz.

CONTENT AND MEDIA: THE HONDA DREAM FACTORY

Audiences respond best when there is new and interesting content to talk about: topics, events, stories about people, information about product developments. Strong content fuels your advertising and extends your media opportunities.

Magazines, newspapers, TV channels and radio stations are always looking for new ways to attract their audiences, too, so the benefits go both ways. As a creative, you want to make the most of your client's initiatives, as well as suggest new ideas that fit their core values.

Discussing these ideas with your client and your media people can expand and deepen your campaign.

Honda is focused on inventive individuals as well as product innovation, and the Honda Dream Factory is a perfect expression of their core values.

W+K ran a 10-part series of advertising features in collaboration with *The Guardian*, describing this 'collective of forward-thinking, inspirational people from the worlds of science, technology, art and culture, all of whom have harnessed the power of dreams to truly innovate in their chosen fields'. You can follow their stories online and visit the Honda Dream Factory website from which the description below is taken. There is advertising for Honda cars on the Dream Factory website. By creating interesting content, the site gives the target audience a good reason to visit and return to it.

It creates another platform for the brand, linked to 'The Power of Dreams'.

WHAT IS THE DREAM FACTORY?

Everyone has a dream, some goal or activity that gives their life deeper meaning and sparks passion.

When we pursue our dreams, we feel empowered. This power, in turn, connects us to others who share the same dreams. It gives us the strength to overcome great challenges. It inspires us to spread the joy of our dreams to other people. Ultimately, the power born of a dream is a creative force, capable of producing revolutionary ideas. http://hub.honda.co.uk/dreamfactory/news-blog-article-pages/

IDENTIFYING THE 'WHEN' OF ADVERTISING

Choosing the best moment to speak to someone often helps you get the response you hope for. If a person is too busy, too tired, or concentrating on finishing their report late on a Friday evening, he or she will either ignore your ad, or it will interrupt their train of thought, but not in a good way. Catch that same person on Saturday morning, over a leisurely breakfast and a relaxing cup of coffee, and their reaction to the same communication could be the opposite. Totally positive.

But when is the best moment? Not just in their day, but in the week, and time of year. And which medium offers you the opportunity to reach someone when they are most receptive? In fact, is it better for advertising to relinquish the notion of controlling the moment, now that the consumer can choose, in so many cases,

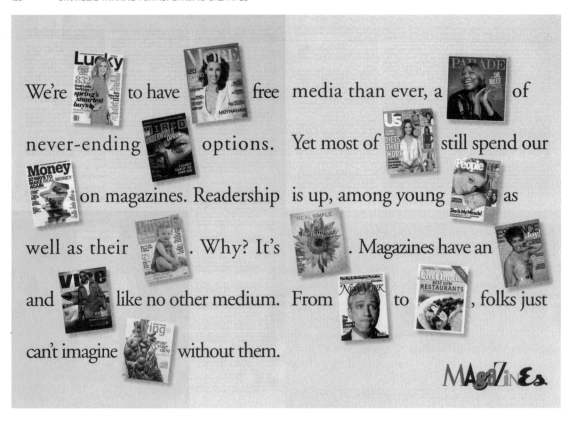

when to engage with your advertising?

These are not simple questions with simple answers. From your own experience, as well as from the campaigns we have looked at so far, you can see that no single medium achieves everything. Together with your media planner, you can and should try to identify a good moment to reach someone, and choose the best medium to do that. You also need to provide a medium for your audience to reach you. That's the advantage of choosing a multi-channel approach in a digital world.

MAKE IT A TWO-WAY CONVERSATION

Reaching your audience most effectively involves a two-way conversation. You can reach your audience with TV, posters, sponsorship, product placement – media that are effective at building strong brands which people trust – such as the ones we have been exploring throughout the book: Apple, Araldite, Cadbury, Duracell, *The Economist*, Evian, the *Financial Times*, Highland Spring, Honda, Lego, L'Oréal, Marmite, Sainsbury's, and more.

Equally, your audience should be able to access elements of your client's offerings, ideally whenever they want to, whether online – through websites, social media, or online magazines and newspapers – via apps, or within paper-based media such as a favourite magazine or newspaper, which are not as time-sensitive as TV or radio.

The ad at the top of the page on the power of print in the US shows how each medium has its shortcomings and benefits. Explore them all with your creativity.

This US ad from the Association of Magazine Media celebrates the rise of magazine readership in the previous five years. According to the association's research, 'The top 25 magazines continue to reach a wider audience than the top 25 prime-time TV shows. And, despite the escalating war for consumers' eyeballs, readers spend an average of 43 minutes per issue'.

MEDIA REQUIREMENT FOR YOUR FIGURE 8 CAMPAIGN

You haven't created your advertising yet, so you might not be sure exactly what media would reach Mark most effectively. Since it should be a two-way conversation, think how you can provide Mark with a way to connect with Figure 8. Make a start, and then add to, or adjust, your media plan once you've created your campaign.

Begin by looking at how you imagined Mark's day, which you described in the third section of 'Who Are You?' You need to connect with him again on that level to see when and where he is likely to be receptive to your advertising. If he's rushing off to work in the morning, does he catch the news online as he drinks his coffee? Banner ads might attract his attention. Or would he block them? What about breakfast TV?

Think about when he's coming home at night, stopping off at the supermarket to pick up some milk. What about in-store promotions? Posters, or an in-store video. Does Mark go to the gym? What could you link with that experience which he would associate with the increased energy he will get from the protein in Figure 8?

Do you have an idea for an app that would attract him – perhaps a branded game, like the VW virtual racing game? What is the essence of the experience that Figure 8 provides for Mark? If it's increased physical energy, running or cycling might be a better activity around which to develop an app. Think about magazines and posters. Mark might read *Men's Health*. He also walks past poster sites. The *FT* used key commuter sites for their campaign, in addition to an interactive online site, branded taxis and direct mail. Postcards can be effective. Mark might pick one up at the cinema. And speaking of cinema, what about product placement? If he saw Figure 8 in a film or TV episode, casually being enjoyed for breakfast by a guy rather than a girl – or by both – that could attract his attention.

What does all this cost? Look at the following campaign by former students, with their accompanying media rationale and media plan. Then make a plan of your own, using whatever information is useful and include it in your brief. Do your own research as well. Since it is impossible to fix certain costs, such as sponsorship and apps, plan what you would like to do, write a rationale, and imagine you have about £2 million to spend. A weekend supplement is an ideal medium for this campaign. Maybe for yours, too. You need to give some information to Mark about the protein in Figure 8. Posters should have no more than ten words, so that's not a good medium for much copy. Websites, banner ads and magazine and press campaigns are all ideal for conveying information.

P&O FERRIES CREATIVE BRIEF

PRODUCT/ SERVICE
P&O Ferries.

OBJECTIVE
To convince non-ferry customers that P&O Ferries is a credible alternative to travelling to Europe with low-cost airlines.

TARGET MARKET
British families who are non-ferry customers, considering European travel in spring/summer.

STRATEGY
By highlighting to families how the inconvenience and discomfort of air travel makes journeying with P&O Ferries a far more enjoyable means of reaching their holiday destination.

PROPOSITION
P&O Ferries – Cruise into holiday mode.

SUPPORT
1. Air travel can be claustrophobic, cramped and uncomfortable.
Onboard a P&O ferry, families aren't confined to a seat for hours on end and can enjoy the freedom of strolling around on deck in the fresh air, so they can arrive at their destination feeling relaxed and refreshed.

2. Airplane food is notoriously bad and unsubstantial.
There are numerous cafes and restaurants and bars onboard a P&O Ferry, offering a wide variety of good quality food so that everyone in the family is catered for.

3. P&O Ferries provide onboard entertainment including live shows, kids' club, cinema screenings and arcade games.
Families are kept amused throughout their journey, meaning the kids won't get restless and irritable and the journey is a fun, enjoyable experience.

4. P&O Ferries is one of Europe's largest, most recognised ferry operators and has won numerous industry awards, including 'World's Leading Ferry Operator'.
Non-ferry customers can take comfort in the fact that P&O Ferries are a trustworthy, well-established brand.

5. There are a number of shops onboard.
Passengers can spend time browsing the shops at their leisure and stock up on last-minute holiday essentials.

COMPETITION
Low-cost airlines – including easyJet, Jet2 and Ryanair, other ferry companies and Eurostar.

MANDATORY
P&O logo.

TONE OF VOICE
Reassuring, friendly, fun.

DESIRED CONSUMER RESPONSE
'I had never really considered going on holiday by ferry – but gosh, it seems like a dream compared to faffing about at airports for hours with the kids!'

MEDIA REQUIREMENT
Press (including newspapers and newspaper supplements) and billboards.

P&O FERRIES MEDIA RATIONALE

Establishing P&O Ferries as a credible alternative to travelling with low-cost airlines can only be achieved by communicating a consistent advertising message through the use of appropriate, relevant media to effectively engage with the target market.

What are the appropriate media?

P&O Ferries is one of Europe's largest, most recognized ferry operators, and is one of the UK's strongest brands. As a well-established company, P&O Ferries enjoy a national presence and a loyal customer base; however, there is still a large proportion of the family market that opt to travel to Europe with low-cost airlines and who have a negative perception of ferry travel.

We believe that with a national advertising campaign that highlights the current disruptions and inconveniences of air travel, while emphasizing the benefits of travelling by ferry, P&O Ferries can commandeer a good proportion of this lucrative family market.

The national campaign that we propose will span three months, from February 1st to April 30th. We feel the timing of this campaign is imperative to its success.

As the majority of British families begin planning their summer holidays (for the July/ August period) within the first part of the year, it is important for P&O Ferries to ensure they are front of mind during this booking period.

We have devised three phases of this 12.5-week campaign which consists of the following media:

Phase 1 – Initial billboard execution to appear for two weeks on 500 sites nationally.

Phase 2 – Three press executions, each one to appear twice in national press every fortnight for 12 weeks.

Phase 3 – Final billboard execution to appear for 2 weeks on 500 sites nationally.

To ensure maximum impact, we feel that the national campaign should be kicked off with an impactful billboard that will appear nationally, across 500 sites. We call this Phase 1 of the campaign. The purpose of this is that by communicating an instant, highly impactful message, we will cut through the visual noise of our target market's daily routine and spark interest in the P&O brand. We also believe that running a highly visual ad about holidaying, while our target market battles through the first few weeks of a miserable British February, will engage with them on an emotional level.

One group who are most likely to be attracted to the service that P&O Ferries offer, are working parents. Therefore they are out and about, they are active and they are using public transport to get to and from work and to travel around urban areas. For this reason we have selected a national package of 500 billboard sites, covering 248 towns through Clear Channel. These sites will be posted at the beginning of February and will run for two weeks. Fifty-nine per cent of these billboards are illuminated, maximizing the visual impact of the P&O ad.

To ensure a constant brand presence, we propose overlapping Phase 1 (Billboard 1) with full-page colour press ads (Phase 2). We would advise that a broader variety of national publications be considered as our target market is quite diverse in their reading. However, with the specified budget firmly in mind we have selected three, cost-effective national titles with high circulation that we believe are well targeted towards our audience.

Our first choice of publication in which we propose to advertise is *The Daily Mail* Weekend Supplement. As our target market are busy, working parents we believe we will be more effective in engaging with them at the weekend when they have more time to spend reading newspapers and magazines. During their leisure time, when they are making plans as a family, they are also more likely to be receptive of our message about booking a family summer holiday. *The Daily Mail* readership fits our target demographic and has a high circulation of 2,006,952 nationally, optimizing the opportunity for P&O Ferries to communicate with a large and appropriate audience.

The second publication we recommend P&O Ferries feature in is *The Guardian* Travel Supplement. As another weekend title, the benefits are the same as advertising in *The Daily Mail* Weekend Supplement. However, as this magazine is more specifically focused on travel, it is likely its readers are considering booking a holiday and so would be in a great mindset to consider P&O Ferries as a viable means of getting there. Even if they're not actively considering going on holiday, the very nature of the travel supplement works in P&O Ferries' favour as it promotes travel and instigates an emotional aspiration for the reader/our target market to escape abroad.

Thirdly, to engage with our target market as they go about their tedious commute to work, and to tie in nicely with the billboards of Phase 1, we propose a full-page colour press ad be placed in *METRO*. The purpose of this is to directly target our working parents as they travel to work via bus, train or tram. This is usually a fairly unpleasant journey and we feel that this is a good time to communicate a fun, friendly message about holidays – a million miles away from their doom and gloom.

METRO is a free, well-established paper read by commuters across 32 UK cities with a circulation of 1,332,192 and an even greater readership. We recommend that P&O Ferries are specific about featuring in *METRO* on a Friday as this is when our target market are thinking ahead to the weekend, making plans about what to do with the kids, etc. Family and leisure time is at the front of their minds and so they are more likely to be receptive to P&O Ferries' message.

METRO readers will have also been well exposed to the initial billboard, so the medium of press allows us to take advantage of this awareness and go into further detail about P&O Ferries as a well-established, trusted company and about the facilities available onboard.

The press coverage will span 12 weeks ensuring the campaign maintains its momentum. Due to restrictions of the advertising budget, this allows for three different executions to appear twice in each of the three publications listed above. So every fortnight P&O Ferries will appear in *The Daily Mail* Weekend Supplement, *The Guardian* Travel Supplement and *METRO*. And every other fortnight there will be a new execution of the campaign. We have selected all of these publications as we feel they share the appropriate tone of voice and taste level for the P&O Ferries brand. They also fit our target market's social classification and age demographic, without being too narrowly specific.

We feel that in the 11th week P&O Ferries can maximize the effectiveness of their campaign by again taking out a national package of 500 billboards. This will act as an impactful reminder message and overlaps with the final press execution.

In summary we believe that a three-month campaign across billboard and press media is the best way for P&O Ferries to engage with their target market. The two billboard executions will nicely sandwich the press ads, acting first to spark interest and then as a reminder. We don't feel that radio is a medium that P&O Ferries should at this moment consider, as this campaign is a very visual one. It is important to note that all of these executions can be adapted to different formats, so should the future budget allow, we feel that they could easily be rolled out as transport posters, bus sides and adshels, etc. We also feel that the TV format would lend itself well to the nature of this campaign, yet this is unachievable within the specified budget.

MEDIA SCHEDULE:

Based on five executions (two x billboards and three x press ads) spanning three months from February 1st to April 30th.

TOTAL = £1, 000, 000

Phase 1 of campaign.
Starting 1st February for two weeks.

Clear Channel:

Type	Coverage	Sites	Exposure	Cost
48-sheet	National	500	Two weeks	£227, 000

TOTAL £227, 000

Phase 2 of campaign.
Weekend supplements

Daily Mail **Weekend Supplement**

Date	Cost per insertion	Accumulative sum
13/02	£41,970	£41,970
27/02	£41,970	£83,940
13/03	£41,970	£125,910
27/03	£41,970	£167,880
10/04	£41,970	£209,850
24/04	£41,970	£251,820
SUBTOTAL	£251,820	

The Guardian **Travel Supplement**

Date	Cost per insertion	Accumulative sum
13/02	£15,300	£15,300
27/02	£15,300	£30,600
13/03	£15,300	£45,900
27/03	£15,300	£61,200
10/04	£15,300	£76,500
24/04	£15,300	£91,800
SUBTOTAL	£91,800	

National Press

Metro

Date	Cost per insertion	accumulative sum
13/02/10	£36,104.60	£36,105
27/02/10	£36,104.60	£72,209.20
13/03/10	£36,104.60	£108,313.80
27/03/10	£36,104.60	£144,418.40
10/04/10	£36,104.60	£180,523.00
24/04/10	£36,104.60	£216,627.60
SUBTOTAL	£216,628	

Press coverage:

£ 251,820 + £91,800 + £216,628 =		£560,248
TOTAL	£560,248	

Phase 3 of campaign.
Starting 16th April for two weeks.

Clear Channel:

Type	Coverage	Sites	Exposure	Cost
48-sheet	National	500	Two weeks	£227,000

TOTAL £227,000

£14,248 overspend.

This is a competitive stance against the low-cost airline experience. The landscape format adds to the relaxing feel of the ad. Think about every aspect of your media, even the shape.

The poster campaign that Roz Waud and Dan Lepännen suggest is a breath of fresh air in late winter when families are looking forward to a holiday. The cost for a national campaign is on their media breakdown.

Share the view, not your armrest.

Cruise into holiday mode. TWO Ferries

YOUR OWN CREATIVE BRIEF FOR DR. MARTENS

In addition to working on the yoghurt brief, you'll also start to work on your own creative brief. The product is Dr. Martens, an English vintage fashion brand that celebrated its fiftieth anniversary in 2010. You might be wearing a pair of Dr. Martens boots right now! Take a fresh worksheet and start to make notes on what you already know, and what more you need to find out. Choose a strategic approach that you think provides the best springboard for your creative work.

It's good practice to go from shaping your own brief to creating a fully-fledged campaign. That's what you'll be doing when putting together your portfolio to show to agencies. Then go ahead with it and do a campaign. Have fun. No one's looking.

THE CLIENT'S PROBLEM

The target audience buys only one pair of Dr. Martens boots, and they last for years. Here's a photo of the originator of the brand, Dr Klaus Maertens, who designed a pair of boots with air-conditioned soles to aid his recovery from an ankle injury sustained while skiing. The other man in the picture, Dr Herbert Funck, helped him improve them.

1   This ad ran in February 2011 in *Grazia* magazine. Imagine that your agency has just won the account. The client wants to attract the same target market but change the approach.

2   Knowing the heritage of a brand can give you fresh ideas. It doesn't mean you have to go down a nostalgia route.

Note:
If you have trouble finding an example of Dr. Martens boots where you live, and you want to be able to try them on to help you work on this brief, you can choose a brand of boots or shoes that approaches the same target market and adapt the brief to suit that product.

3   Had the client presented this years ago, you might not have imagined there was a way to create a cutting-edge, fashionable image for such a workmanlike pair of boots.

1

2

OBSERVATION IS PART OF RESEARCH

See how much research you can do even without sophisticated tracking studies, and other data to which you would have access in an agency. You can research the product and its potential audience by going to a store and trying on the boots, talking to the shop assistants, and asking your friends what they like (or don't like) about the product.

Asking people you don't know is useful, too. Write a few questions down and see if you can do an informal interview in a shop, if the owner doesn't mind! Take note of what people say. Write it down. A casual remark can sometimes turn into a great headline.

Think about what the main competition is. What would a person buy instead of a pair of Dr. Martens boots? Who is the primary audience? Do you think the best solution to the client's problem is to attract a wider audience to the brand, or to persuade current fans to buy more than one pair of boots?

Which product should you feature? You could, for example, use their fiftieth anniversary (2010) as a starting point. They made a limited-edition pair of red Dr. Martens boots to celebrate. If you decide to go down that route, see what the boots look like, and put that into the first section of your creative brief as the 'product'. And go from there.

You can change your mind, cross out, start again. It's a work in progress and it's all up to you. You'll experience what it's like to forge a creative brief and make decisions on your own.

When you come to the specific section called 'strategy', try thinking of several possible options. There is no single 'right' strategy. Try to make yours as distinctive as you can. That will make your advertising more creative and more memorable.

Remember to keep working on this brief as you go through each chapter.

CONCLUSION

We began the final chapter with a coffee – the Starbucks app – and to close the conversation, perhaps it's time for a beer.

Here is an inventive strategic approach for Bud Ice from Budweiser's agency, TribalDDB. It's a simple message: 'the hotter the day, the less you pay'.

This campaign makes use of a simple device which tells you the temperature. And when the temperature goes over a certain threshold, you get a free pint at one of the participating pubs. Again, the app works as an advertising tool and as a means of increasing revenue for the pubs – presumably for Bud Ice if you like the beer.

This campaign ran in Ireland only, on TV and digital, on social media via Facebook, and it works via this app. Everyone always wonders what the temperature is. And when it's hot, you get thirsty. It's engaging.

It's the kind of thing that shows an understanding of how to make multi-platform media work for a specific place, season and person. It would be a perfect project to put in your portfolio to show that you can think strategically and originate a creative solution in a difficult and highly competitive category. Cheers!

CREATIVE BRIEF TEMPLATE

1
PRODUCT / SERVICE
What, precisely, is your advertising selling?

2
OBJECTIVE
What must your advertising achieve?

3
TARGET MARKET
Who is the primary focus of your advertising?

4
STRATEGY
How will the advertising achieve its task?

5
PROPOSITION
What's the 'hook' that will attract the target market? Write it in one clear sentence.
This is invaluable as your work-in-progress campaign line—or as your final one.

6

SUPPORT

Why does the product interest this target market? List in order of importance, turning the attributes into benefits wherever possible.

1

2

3

7

COMPETITION

Who else is fighting for your target market's attention in this area?

8

MANDATORY

What has to appear in the advertising—e.g., a legal requirement.

9

TONE OF VOICE

Describe the campaign's character—in three adjectives, max!

10

DESIRED CONSUMER RESPONSE

What do you want your target to do, feel, or think after seeing the advertising.

11

MEDIA REQUIREMENT

Where will the advertising appear?

WHO ARE YOU TEMPLATE?

1
DESCRIBE THE PERSON YOU ARE TALKING TO.

It could be someone you know, or you could create an imaginary character. It has to be someone interested in your proposition Give this person a good name, so that you have a clear picture in your mind.

WHO ARE THEY?

Where do they live and who do they live with?

What job do they do?

What are their hobbies/interests?

WHAT DO THEY LIKE?

Tastes, list of likes and dislikes

2
DECIDE WHAT YOU WANT TO SAY

What promise or benefit can you offer that you believe will genuinely interest the person you've described. Don't try to be clever at this point. You're not writing copy, just deciding what is your best offer. If you don't have a unique selling point, look for the emotional selling point. Write as clearly and briefly as you can, in a conversational tone.

IMAGINE PRECISELY HOW AND WHERE THE PROMISE OR BENEFIT YOU'RE PRESENTING CONNECTS WITH THE PERSON YOU'RE TALKING TO

Where will he or she receive your message as the day unfolds. What mood will this person be in when your message reaches them? You could draw a graph of their day. Now you'll begin to see how the product or service you have to offer fits into that individual's life. Once you understand this, you're ready to write good copy.

TYPICAL WEEKDAY OR WEEKEND

Look at a typical weekday or weekend in the subject's life and then below plot out the media that they will come into contact with, depending on the product/service you are advertising .

MEDIA THAT HE OR SHE WILL COME INTO CONTACT WITH

Billboards, branded content, cinema, experiential events, product placement
Online media, mobile apps
Magazines/newspapers
TV and radio

FURTHER READING

As a creative person you will want to immerse yourself in every branch of the arts and media as never-ending sources of inspiration and information. D&AD and One Show Annuals are all valuable and enjoyable to dip into. In addition, here is a selection of useful, well-written, specialized books which are well worth your time. Some are closely related to strategy, while others focus on equally vital topics, such as Simon Veksner's *How to Make It As An Advertising Creative.*

Aitchison, Jim, *Cutting Edge Advertising*, Prentice Hall, 1999.

Alder, Harry, *Mind to Mind Marketing, Communicating with 21ˢᵗ-century Customers*, Kogan Page Ltd, 2001.

Altstiel, Tom and Grow, Jean, *Advertising Creative: Strategy, Copy + Design*, Sage Publications, Inc., 2010.

Berns, Gregory, *Satisfaction, the Science of Finding True Fulfillment*, Henry Holt & Company, 2005.

Bullmore, Jeremy, *Behind the Scenes in Advertising*, second edition, Admap Publications, UK. 1998.

Butterfield, Leslie (ed.), *Excellence in Advertising*, Butterworth, Heinemann, 1997.

Cooper, Alan (ed.), *How to Plan Advertising*, second edition, Continuum, 2001.

Gladwell, Malcolm, *Blink*, Penguin, 2005.

Hegarty, John, *Hegarty on Advertising*, Thames & Hudson, 2011.

Law, Andy, *Open Minds*, Orion Business Books, 1999.

Lehrer, Jonah, *How We Decide*, Houghton Mifflin Harcourt, 2010.

Lowe, Frank, *Dear Lord Leverhulme, I Think We May Have Solved Your Problem*, Hurtwood Press Limited, 2002.

Lucas, Gavin and Dorrian, Mike, *Guerrilla Advertising: Unconventional Brand Communication*, Laurence King Publishing, 2006.

Lucas, Gavin and Dorrian, Mike, *Guerrilla Advertising 2: More Unconventional Brand Communication*, Laurence King Publishing, 2011

Thaler, Richard and Sunstein, Cass, *Nudge, Improving Decisions about Health, Wealth and Happiness*, Yale University Press, 2008.

Timmers, Margaret (ed.), *The Power of the Poster*, V&A Publications, 1998.

Tovstiga, George, *Strategy in Practice*, John Wiley and Sons, Ltd., 2010.

Veksner, Simon, *How to Make It As An Advertising Creative*, Laurence King Publishing, 2010.

INDEX

Page numbers in *italics* refer to illustrations

PICTURE CREDITS

Laurence King Publishing Ltd wish to thank the following companies, institutions and individuals who have kindly provided photographic material for use in this book. Numbers below are page numbers. While every effort has been made to trace the present copyright holders, we apologise in advance for any unintentional omission or error and will be pleased to insert the appropriate acknowledgement in any subsequent edition.

pp.9–10 Volkswagen AG. The copyright is reserved to Volkswagen AG. p.12 Client: *The Economist*; Agency: AMVBBDO. p.13 Creative Directors: Simon Dicketts and Graham Fink; Copy Writers: Simon Dicketts – 'Sandals' (yellow) – 'Piers' (Green), Orlando Warner – 'Middle England' (White); Art Director: Graham Fink; Planner: Neil Godber; Media Planner: Richard Evans; Director/ photographer/illustrator: Gareth Davies. p.16 British Egg Information Service. p.21 Creative team: Freddie Wood and Stephanie Forbe - Creative Team. p.25 Ros Chast/The New Yorker. p.27 Agency: Ogilvy France; Copywriter: Fergus O'Hare; Art-Director: Ginevra Capece; Designers: Sid Tomkins, Tanya Holbrook; Illustrator: Noma Bar; Creative Director: Susan Westre; Account Managers: Ben Messiaen, Eléonore Di Perno. pp.28–29 Creative Director: Lorenzo Marini; Art Director: Paolo Bianchini; Copywriter: Elisa Maino; Client: Stella - Officine Metallurgiche Lux; Product: Espresso coffee maker. p.31 Lapiz USA, Leo Burnett/Procter & Gamble. pp.32–33 The Gillette Company. p.35 Innocent Drinks Ltd. p.36l Courtesy of GE. p.36r. Innocent Drinks Ltd. p.37 ©Legambiente. pp.38–39 The Hymn of Doing Heimat/Hornbach. p.41 Mini UK. pp.43–45 Volkswagen AG. The copyright is reserved to Volkswagen AG. p.49 Courtesy Fiat. p.50 Courtesy American Airlines. p.52 © The foundation for a better life. www.values.com; Photo: Russ Dixon Photography.com. p.55 ©Alan Brooking/DDB UK. p.56 ADESF. p.59 Renfe. p.60 Courtesy Fiat; actor: Peter Aubery. p.62 ©Apple Inc. Use with permission. All rights reserved. Apple® and the Apple logo are registered trademark of Apple Inc. p.64 *The Independent*. p.67 Samsonite International S.A. p.69 Campaign created by Joe Talboys and Anouk Robert. p.70 Courtesy Lakeland. p.72l © Charles Schwab & Co., Inc. p.72r Courtesy Citibank. p.73t © Intuit Inc. All rights reserved. Intuit, the Intuit Logo, and Small Business, Rejoice are trademarks of Intuit Inc. p.73b Cover courtesy - Photography D. Venni at red Represent/Hearst Rodale. p.75 Nick Worthington: Colenso BBDO Executive Creative Director; Levi Slavin: Colenso BBDO Creative Director; Kia Heinnen & Zoe Hawkins: Colenso BBDO Art Director/Copywriter; Lisa Fedyszyn & Jonathin Mcmahon: Colenso BBDO Creatives; Lou Kuegler: Colenso BBDO Group Account Director; Marcelle Baker: Colenso Senior Account Director; Celeste Pulman: Colenso BBDO Account Director; Dave Munn: Colenso BBDO Account Director; Dave Munn: Colenso BBDO Senior Account Manager; Alex Swney: Heart of the City CEO; Jane Stewart: Heart of the City Project Manager; Tash Stitchbury: Heart of the City Project Manager. p.79 Bric's; Artistic Director: Alberto Tandoi. p.80 Created by Audience Technologies & Insight at Channel 4 Television Corporation, working in partnership with Crowd DNA. www.channel4sales.com, www.crowddna. com. pp.85–86 Ed Ryder and Bryan Stewart. p.89 Volkswagen AG. The copyright is reserved to Volkswagen AG. p.90 Creative Directors: Simon Dicketts and Graham Fink; Copy Writers: Simon Dicketts – 'Sandals' (Yellow) – 'Piers' (Green); Orlando Warner – 'Middle England' (White); Art Director: Graham Fink; Planner: Neil Godber; Media planner: Richard Evans; Director/ photographer/illustrator: Gareth Davies. p.91 Courtesy BBH/ Levi Strauss & Co. pp.92–93 Agency: BETC Euro RSCG; Agency Account Management: Marielle Durandet / Dominique Verot Catherine Clement / Marie-Josee Cadorette; Global Creative Director: Remi Babinet; Art Director: Agnes Cavard; Assistant Art Director: Gregory Ferembach; Copywriter: Valerie Chidiovsky; TV Producer: Fabrice Brovelli; Music Supervisor: Christophe Caurret; Music Production: BETC Music; Production Company: Partizan; Director: Michael Gracey. p.95 Agency: BETC Euro RSCG; Account team: Marielle Durandet, Dominique Verot, Gaelle Gicqueau, Isabelle Picot, Marie-Josee Cadorette, Antoine Clemenceau; Global Creative Director: Remi Babinet; Art Director: Agnes Chidlovdky; Art Director Assistant: Gregory Ferembach; Art Buyer: Nathalie Gruselle; Images: Photographer: Nathaniel Goldberg, Photographer of the babies: Valerie Mathilde, Photographic Assistants: John Guerrero, Nicholas Kengen & Julie Meresse; Production & Editing: Rita Production Manager, Karine Manzie Production Coordinator, Jamila Wahid. p.96 Courtesy ADESF. p.99 Courtesy Unilever. p.103 LOREAL. P.104 Ed Ryder and Bryan Stewart. p.105 Jeremy Bullmore. p.106 LEGO: Christian Korbes, Vice President, Marketing, LEGO Central Europe; Katharina Sutch, PR & Communications Director, CE-Brand Marketng; Agency: serviceplan campaign 1 gmbh; Executive Creative Director: Oliver Palmer; Text/Copywriter: Frank Seiler; Art Director: Sandra Loibl, Julia Koch; Account Management: Monika Klingenfuss/ Denise Mancinone; Graphic Design: Franc Rofischer; Fotografie/Illustration: Susanne Dittrich,

ACKNOWLEDGEMENTS

Many thanks to my colleagues and former students who so generously contributed their knowledge, time and talent throughout the course of this book.

Lucy Alexander, for her expert advice on Channel 4's research on Tribes; Digby Atkinson for his inside knowledge of the launch of *The Independent*; Jeremy Bullmore for all that I learned from him, and for permission to include material from his excellent book; Alastair Crompton for offering me the rare opportunity of a second career; Rob Kitchen for his explanation, and images, of the Araldite campaign; Mike Murphy for permission to use his beautifully art-directed Duracell posters, and for his help with screengrabs of digital work. I'd also like to thank my daughter Josie for tracking and analyzing her response to aspects of social media.

Special thanks to each of the following creatives, whose inventive work has illuminated key sections of the book: Stef Forbes, Pete Gosselin, Jay Hunt, Dan Leppänen, Will Lowe, Victor Monclus, Anouk Robert, Ed Ryder, Bryan Stewart, Joe Talboys, Roz Waud, and Fred Wood. Limitation of space prevented more campaigns from being included. My thanks to Adarsha Deshbhratar, Nathan Bradley, Felipe Guimaraes, Marissia Thomadaki and Becky Wass for taking the time to offer and prepare their excellent work. I am grateful, also, to Ruby Harrison for sharing her notes from London Week, including a key quote from the charismatic Dan Watts, at Fallon: 'Strategy is 70% of creativity'.

Sincere thanks to my editors at Laurence King: Jo Lightfoot who understood the potential of making strategic thinking the subject of a book, rather than a mere chapter within one; Anne Townley who helped me cut and shape the material; and Peter Jones who saw the book smoothly through to its completion.

Many thanks to Jo St. Mart, whose tireless picture research produced such positive results.

Jane Turnbull, my agent, has been, as ever, an extraordinary source of support.

An enormous thank you to my husband and first reader, Fred Taylor, whose IT skills proved invaluable, as well as his fluent German, and of course, his loving patience.